Luigi Wewege and Michael C. Thomsett
The Digital Banking Revolution

Luigi Wewege and Michael C. Thomsett

The Digital Banking Revolution

How Fintech Companies Are Transforming
the Retail Banking Industry Through
Disruptive Financial Innovation

3rd edition

DE GRUYTER

A large portion of the proceeds from the sale of this book will go toward funding the Luigi Wewege Foundation, which provides an annual academic scholarship to a deserving American student. For more information, please visit: www.luigiwewegefoundation.com.

For any comments, suggestions or feedback, please contact the author via: info@digitalbankingrevolution.com.

ISBN 978-1-5474-1833-6
e-ISBN (PDF) 978-1-5474-0159-8
e-ISBN (EPUB) 978-1-5474-0161-1

Library of Congress Control Number: 2019949227

Bibliographic information published by the Deutsche Nationalbibliothek
The Deutsche Nationalbibliothek lists this publication in the Deutsche Nationalbibliografie; detailed bibliographic data are available on the Internet at http://dnb.dnb.de.

© 2020 Luigi Wewege and Michael C. Thomsett
Published by Walter de Gruyter Inc., Boston/Berlin
Cover image: antoniokhr/iStock/Getty Images Plus
Typesetting: Integra Software Services Pvt. Ltd.
Printing and binding: CPI books GmbH, Leck

www.degruyter.com

This book is dedicated to my amazing parents, Desmond and Loretta Wewege, without whom none of my success would have been possible!

– Luigi Wewege

Many thanks to the talented and dedicated editors of the world for diligently pursuing excellence and accuracy in all that they publish. These are the unsung heroes of the publishing world.

– Michael C. Thomsett

Praise for the Book

The Digital Banking Revolution *captures the effects of disruption brought to the banking industry by emergent financial technology businesses. The authors provide a fascinating examination of several companies who have recently developed new financial innovations and how they are demonstrably significant to the consumer.*

Victor von Gierszewski
Managing Director
TNS Global

The Digital Banking Revolution *provides a unique take on the consumerization of retail banking services. It elucidates on how banks are facing increasing pressure from digital competitors, and how by recognizing these threats they can now go on the offensive by developing innovative technologies of their own.*

Reginald D. Jele
Chief of Staff to the Minister of Finance
Republic of South Africa

The Digital Banking Revolution *should be considered a survival guide for bank leaders, providing those in the industry with a strategic blueprint on how to adapt, evolve and succeed in this digital age.*

G. Paul Warner
Former Private Bank Director
National Australia Bank

The Digital Banking Revolution *is an informative read focused on the transformational changes facing traditional retail banks worldwide. It covers insightful well-researched analysis on: big data, customer engagement, disruptive technologies, mobile payments, and the changing financial behaviors of consumers, in particular millennials.*

Michael A. C. Hart
Chairman and CEO
TPS Capital

The Digital Banking Revolution *is an insightful look at how financial technology has brought welcome changes to the banking industry. This is essential reading not only for the next generation of retail bank customers, but also for those who want to fully understand how financial services will be conducted going forward.*

Thomas J. O'Rourke
Assistant Director, Banking
The Bermuda Monetary Authority

https://doi.org/10.1515/9781547401598-202

The Digital Banking Revolution *book is an absolute must read for those who wish to gain a deeper understanding of how innovative technologies are shaping the future of financial services.*

Boris Simic
Director DACH
Klarna Inc.

Foreword

For many years, retail banks have been secure, highly profitable businesses. However, recent industry disruption has come knocking at the door of these financial giants. The turning point was the global financial crisis experienced between the years 2007–2009, which not only led to large losses, and even the collapse of a significant number of established banks, but shook the trust of financial customers worldwide. These factors, combined with the fact that banking has been relatively undisturbed for centuries, meant it was time for change, and that change has been the rapid rise of financial technology companies, or *fintech*.

Emergent innovative financial technologies are profoundly changing the ways in which we spend, move, and manage our money unlike ever before. The digital transformation and its pace of change have been truly astounding, dramatically shifting customer behaviors and expectations of their financial service providers. Retail banks must now become positioned to fulfill their customers' every financial need, especially as the Millennial generation (those born between the early 1980s and early 2000s) is poised to command the most purchasing power of any age group. Banks will need to become more cognizant of this generation for a multitude of reasons. Research undertaken by the Cassandra Report[1] into how Millennials conduct their financial services has shown a defined trend in that they typically do not have the same legacy relationship with their banks as older generations had. The research indicates that Millennials judge banks based on their digital capabilities and will not hesitate to switch their bank account to another provider if they consider it to offer a better banking service.[2] The overall progress of financial service innovations has been driven by adoption across all age groups, but the demand from the Millennial generation to push the boundaries of innovation and to think about financial services differently has been a major catalyst for disruptive change.

Regional banks impact this changing landscape more than very small or extremely large banking corporations. Most media attention has been focused on the large national banks, of which there are only a handful. In the US, these include four mega-banks: JPMorgan Chase, Bank of America, Citigroup, and Wells Fargo.[3] The medium-sized regional banks, defined by the Federal Reserve as those with assets between $10 billion and $50 billion, have significant impact on how banking truly operates. For example, mega-banks are affected by federal regulation and oversight, and small banks escape that level of scrutiny. Regional bank regulation

---

1 https://cassandra.co/
2 https://blog.accessdevelopment.com/2018-customer-loyalty-statistics#bank
3 https://www.bankrate.com/banking/americas-top-10-biggest-banks/#slide=1

https://doi.org/10.1515/9781547401598-203

falls somewhere in between, and with the ability to operate across state lines since 1994, the situation for regional banks is ideal right now.[4]

There is much more to this analysis, but as a starting point it just makes sense to study the differences between the massive banks that control most of the industry, the small local banks, and the regional banks that operate in more than one state but have a "local" feel which consumers seem to like.[5]

Edwin Carlson

COO/Director of EQITrade (EQIExchange & EQIBank) – the world's first licensed and regulated bank for fiat and digital assets

---

4 https://www.federalreservehistory.org/essays/riegle_neal_act_of_1994

5 Lakshmi Balasubramanyan and Joseph G. Haubrich (2013). "What Do We Know about Regional Banks? An Exploratory Analysis," Federal Reserve Bank of Cleveland, working paper no. 13–16.

Contents

About the Authors

 **Luigi Wewege** is the Senior Vice President and Head of Private Banking of Belize-based Caye International Bank, Principal of Palmetto Global Ventures, a financial consultancy firm focused on digital banking and fintech solutions, and serves as an Instructor at the FinTech School, which provides online training courses on the latest technological and innovation developments within the financial services industry. Outside of his main roles Luigi additionally serves as a Mentor at FinTech Go, a startup accelerator for financial technology companies, as a Team Member of the FinTech Portfolio, the world's 1st member-owned FinTech innovation ecosystem, and as a speaker for the Silicon Valley Innovation Center.

Previously Luigi was the CEO of Vivier & Co, a boutique financial services firm, the Commercial Manager of publicly listed Investment Research Group, a financial advisory company where he led their media division, and was a Senior Consultant at The Braintrust Network, which was a Central Europe-based management consultancy. Notably, while Luigi was completing his undergraduate degree he executed a pilot study for the Federal Trade Commission during one of the most serious financial times for the American economy. The primary focus of the study was to examine and determine the accuracy of credit bureau information. The research he conducted ultimately provided the impetus for a report which was presented before the United States Congress under Section 319 of the Fair and Accurate Credit Transactions Act of 2003.

Luigi holds a Master of Business Administration with a major in international business from the MIB School of Management. He also holds a Bachelor of Science in Business Administration with a triple major in finance, international business, and management *cum laude* from the University of Missouri-St. Louis. While at university Luigi was a multiple recipient of the Dean's list and Coaches and Athletic Director honor rolls, and received the Great Lakes Valley Conference Academic All-Conference honors. Other academic achievements for him include being formally inducted into the Financial Management Association – National Honor Society and the Epsilon Eta Pi – International Business Honor Society. More recently, he was the honored recipient of the Salute to Business Achievement Award, which recognizes outstanding UMSL business alumni.

One of Luigi's passions is to create development opportunities that empower young people to create positive change, and this led him to start his own Foundation, which provides an annual academic scholarship to a deserving American student. Previously he served as a Director and Trustee of Doing Good Fellows, a pioneering non-profit which uses technology to facilitate an ecosystem where accomplished professionals use their skills, and networks to deliver global social impact. Luigi is also the past president of Junior Chamber International (JCI) – Metro, a worldwide youth service organization with members in over 120 countries, and consultative status with the Council of Europe, the United Nations, and UNESCO. The primary focus of Luigi's presidency was to create innovative fundraising initiatives to assist JCI's partnership with the United Nations Foundation and Nothing But Nets campaign, which help prevent malaria deaths by purchasing, distributing, and teaching the proper use of mosquito bed nets throughout Southern Africa.

Outside of work Luigi enjoys participating in a variety of sports, and has competed in several at a high level. Select athletic achievements for him include being a former national junior champion in swimming and a National Collegiate Athletic Association golfer on university scholarship. For more information about Luigi, please visit his personal website: www.luigiwewege.com.

https://doi.org/10.1515/9781547401598-205

 **Michael C. Thomsett** is a professional author of dozens of books on financial and investment topics, as well as several published peer-reviewed papers.

The range of financial topics include investing and trading, business management, and many other topics.

Papers published in journals include:

Review of Management Innovation and Creativity (RMIC):
– Spring, 2011 (Volume 4, Issue 9) – "Global Supply Chain Risk Management: Viewing the Past to Manage Today's Risks from an Historical Perspective"
– Fall, 2011 (Volume 4, Issue 12) – "Business Risks Associated with Aggressive Interpretation of Accounting Guidelines"
International Journal of Accounting Information Science and Leadership:
– Fall, 2011 (Volume 4, Issue 10) – "Security and Financial Valuation Issues Relating to Trade Secrets"
Journal of Information Systems Technology and Planning (JISTP):
– Fall, 2011 (Volume 4, Issue 9) – "Invisible Risks Related to Improved Data Efficiency and Technology"
Journal of Knowledge and Human Resource Management (JKHRM):
– Fall 2011 (Volume 3, Issue 4) – "Risk Management Challenges Regarding Trade Secret Vulnerabilities and Legal Issues"
Journal of Technical Analysis (JOTA):
– July 2017 (Issue 69) – "Signal Correlation Applied to Charting Techniques"

Thomsett's published books include the best-selling *Options* (De Gruyter, 2018). The book has sold over 300,000 copies in its ten editions. He also has published widely through De Gruyter, FT Press, John Wiley & Sons, Amacon, Palgrave Macmillan, and others.

Chapter 1
Introduction

Banks have always fought to gain absolute power and market share, knowing their competition and serving a marketplace that had relatively few alternative choices. However, the battlefield is changing as financial technology advances and new players emerge. Today, financial customers have become restless, demanding more from their financial service providers than ever before. Many retail banks around the world have now reached a pivotal moment in their history, and they need to transform through financial technological advancements to stay relevant, or risk the possibility that agile financial start-ups could confine them to a limited utility role. This challenge comes at an inopportune time for retail banks just as industry profitability is stagnating and customer loyalty is becoming even more tenuous.

Regional banks experience an average of 11% attrition overall, and as much as 20–25% for first-year accounts. One study by consultants Bain & Company concluded that on average, 29% of regional bank customers would change banks if it could be done easily. In fact, the time and effort involved in switching banks is an outstanding reason that many customers do *not* switch banks.[1]

At the same time, regional banking is growing quickly, adding fierce competition to the market, with rapid change continuing to intensify. For example, with narrowing spreads between long-term and short-term lending, profits are being squeezed and regional banks are being forced to streamline their cost and expense levels.[2]

These banking trends are not the same as those of the distant past, when growth had everything to do with increased customer accounts and savings rates. Today, dominated by fintech trends, banking has changed completely.

To illustrate how rapidly new technology can transform an industry, consider that it took just 18 months for Google to erase 85% of the market capitalization of the biggest GPS companies in the world after the launch of its Google Maps app. Alibaba, China's equivalent to Amazon, became that country's largest multinational holding company only nine months after entering the market.

These examples show how today's technology-enabled disruptors can dramatically change markets in a short period. For many, the first real disruptor to enter the banking sector in the current era was PayPal. Initially, traditional banks treated PayPal as an annoyance, limited to eBay and with little potential to disrupt the highly lucrative and bank-dominated payments industry. How wrong they were. At the end of 2018 it had $15.45 billion in revenue, and was more valuable than its parent eBay,

---

1 https://postfunnel.com/drives-loyalty-todays-banking-customers/
2 https://www.wsj.com/articles/regional-banks-brush-off-yield-curve-worries-11547683841

https://doi.org/10.1515/9781547401598-001

which booked $10.75 billion in revenues in 2018 and has been growing at about 8% per year.[3] PayPal revenue for 2019 are estimated to grow to $18 billion. Average revenues are growing at 18% per year.[4]

PayPal has paved the way for the payments space to be transformed, with popular retailers having also shown remarkable success moving into payments. It's all about convenience and speed. Banking under the PayPal model doesn't even require leaving home; and it doesn't end there. For example: the Starbucks Rewards loyalty program handles 30% of the company's United States-based transactions, and 1.9 million new customers signed up to the program in 2018.[5]

These trends are symptoms of what is occurring in the market today, and of the role technology is playing. Previously, a tight regulatory environment acted as a barrier to entry for those who wanted to access the banking industry, but today these barriers have become more relaxed. To illustrate, PayPal has been a licensed bank in Europe since 2007, and Facebook, which has more than 250 million users in Europe, was authorized in late 2018 by the Central Bank of Ireland to handle payments across the entire European Union, through its service, Facebook Pay.[6]

Other new entrants that have grown rapidly without the need for regulation include Google with Google Pay, TransferWise, and SimplePay.[7] Many of these non-bank financial institutions have all relied on similar "white-label" services, such as those offered by The Bancorp, Inc., which is able to provide regulated banking services to its clients' customers. This is accomplished through the development of internal regulatory systems, designed to protect customers without the need for outside oversight. The CEO of The Bancorp explained this concept in 2017:[8]

> As new core team members, these individuals bring game-changing experience to us in the operations and risk management arenas. Their demonstrated, senior-level track records in large, complex institutions give us a greater capacity to reengineer our platform. We have now attained critical mass in our management talent, and are poised for the next phase of transformation that will enhance our platform for clients and spur us toward innovative growth.
>
> **Damian Kozlowski**
> CEO and President

---

3 https://www.macrotrends.net/stocks/charts/EBAY/ebay/revenue and https://www.statista.com/statistics/382619/paypal-annual-revenue/
4 https://www.macrotrends.net/stocks/charts/PYPL/paypal-holdings/revenue
5 https://www.pymnts.com/earnings/2018/starbucks-rewards-mobile-app-stocks-loyalty/
6 https://medium.com/@alena.degrik/facebook-pay-is-planning-to-enter-the-eu-market-will-it-launch-in-ukraine-7f9c4c73a27b
7 https://pay.google.com/about/ -
 https://transferwise.com/us -
 https://www.simplepaygroup.com/
8 https://www.thebancorp.com/about/news/2017/07/team-updates-07262017/

In today's digital world, winning and retaining customers hinges on creating value to enhance convenience and quality beyond mere financial transactions. This marketing strategy is embraced by major digital players such as Apple, Amazon, Alibaba, and Google. For retail banks, this requires a dramatic shift in strategic focus from being a provider of financial products and services to becoming a provider of solutions. Banks cannot respond to these threats by simply being more technologically advanced or reducing the number of branches they operate, but by rolling out better mobile and online banking services.

What banks need to do is first defend their competitive position and learn how to play a greater role, not just at the exact moment of the financial transaction but before and after it as well. For retail banks to regain control in this era of digitization, as well as succeed in an increasingly competitive market, they will need to outsmart and outmaneuver the new financial disruptors, primarily smaller banks growing into a regional presence or new start-up banks.

Disrupters are flexible and able to move quickly. Their products have expanded as well, far beyond traditional banking. These disrupters offer insurance, consulting, financial planning, retirement and estate services, and more. This new range of "value chain" products are competitive with regional banks.

One of the greatest disrupters is the new banking system itself. Banking services are now being provided by the "sharing economy" in which information technology and decentralized assets are replacing traditional banks.

Even blockchain is surging in the banking industry. Though many of the numerous blockchain companies will not likely survive, those that do will compete directly with banks on all levels. The digital economy is becoming the mainstream economy, but many old-style bankers have not recognized this trend.

To the extent that blockchain companies will be able to provide resources for customer service, operational efficiency, and the use of big data, the digital revolution potentially may crush many regional banks, if not others spanning the entire industry. In this new economy, *customer intelligence*—values held by a bank's customers and priorities in service—may become the greatest driver of revenue and profits in the future. The digital banks today have access to more information about customers than brick and mortar banks ever had in the past. Simply stated, this is a profound competitive advantage.

Beyond these market advantages, digital banking will employ robotics and AI to further reduce costs and create even more market advantage. The combined capabilities under this model include analysis of emotional intelligence, logical reasoning, self-supervised learning and training, and pattern recognition that no bank teller will ever be able to duplicate.

Infrastructure will also be remodeled and become dominant, through cloud-based processing. Many institutions already use software-as-a-service (SAAS) for traditional processes such as HR and financial accounting. But this technology is exploding and will quickly dominate consumer payment processing, credit scoring, billings, and current account tracking.

These revolutionary changes will require increased cyber-security, and many institutions already are addressing this. It will take time, however, due to cross-border data transactions, complex new technologies, use of third-party vendor services, new security threats, and the increased use of the internet of things (IoT).

Although this new digital reality is moving quickly, the range of threats facing retail banks is daunting. Figure 1.1 outlines the biggest challenges threatening banks' ability to grow at present in the US marketplace, the world's largest. The remainder of this introduction will focus on the elements of Figure 1.1 as they affect

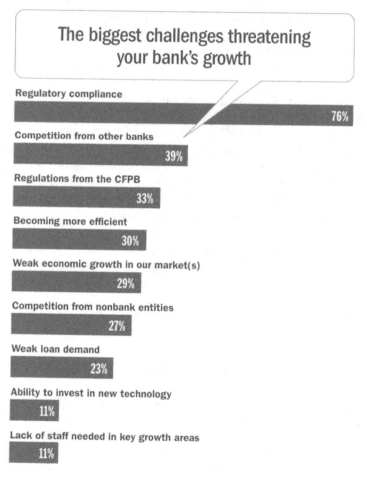

Figure 1.1: The biggest challenges threatening your bank's growth.
Source: Bank Director © September 2015. The Financial Brand.

the US—which is highly regulated and well developed, with local banking being the norm. We will look at how these elements will affect the rest of the world in detail later in the book.

To explore these challenges in more detail, the following sections explain and compare the digital challenges that banks face specifically in the US, but also in the rest of the world.

Regulatory Compliance

Many relatively new reforms and regulations were introduced following enactment of the 2010 Dodd-Frank Wall Street Reform and Consumer Protection Act. Now, nearly a decade later, many lawmakers and regulators are taking another look and identifying sections of Dodd-Frank that could be rolled back or softened. At the same time, some members of Congress have encouraged the House Financial Services Committee to preserve regulations. In other words, it is not certain whether regulations will be amended or kept in place in coming years.

Competition from Other Banks

Most economists believe that competition is a positive force in banking. Regional banks are figuring out how to become more competitive in the years following the 2008–2009 problems in the financial sector overall. Some have learned that it is possible to compete by partnering with fintech companies, developing lending networks to provide alternatives to customers, and building revenue-sharing systems so that banks are able to cooperate with one another rather than compete head to head.

Regulation from the CFPB

The Consumer Financial Protection Bureau (CFPB) enforces a dizzying array of regulations in its oversight role for banks. Compliance demands considerable time and resources.

Within the CFPB's jurisdiction are equal credit opportunity rules, home mortgage disclosure requirements, electronic funds transfers, fair debt collection practices, licensing of mortgage loan originators, disclosure rules for banks not offering Federal Deposit Insurance, rules of practice, fair credit reporting, real estate settlement procedures, truth in lending, and truth in savings, among others.

CFPB regulations go even further, imposing and enforcing regulations about policies and procedures, records, equal access, disabilities, rulemaking, investigations, and official notifications.[9]

Becoming More Efficient

Regional banks have recognized the need to become streamlined and efficient organizations. In an effort to cut costs and enhance profits, regional banks need to critically address several issues. These include optimizing service delivery and even determining whether the number of physical bank branches makes sense. If branches are not profitable, they can be closed. Past standards that "more is better" were based on the assumption that future profits required having more branches, but today this standard does not always make sense.

The application of new technology and improved internal processes also improves efficiency, but past systems, including limiting a labor force, are not as effective as marketing research performed digitally. In this effort, alignment between marketing and resources is improved with digital products for customer identification and services.

Finally, banks can vastly improve efficiency by considering how they may outsource services that are expensive to offer directly. Just as it no longer makes sense to open new branches for the sake of the numbers, it also does not make sense to strive for all-inclusive services offered at the branch level. The digital banking world defies this assumption.

Weak Economic Growth in Our Market(s)

The financial industry may experience long-term gradual declines in the economic cycle. This is caused by reductions in consumer spending and borrowing, uncertainty about the future housing market and interest rates, slowing business investment, trade tensions, tariffs and balance of trade problems, and the possibility of economic impacts from government shutdowns or border closures.[10]

---

9 https://www.consumerfinance.gov/policy-compliance/rulemaking/final-rules/code-federal-regulations/
10 https://www.focus-economics.com/regions/major-economies

Competition from Non-bank Entities

The trend toward banking services provided by non-banks, sometimes referred to as the *shadow banking system*, is one of the trends every bank needs to be aware of and contend with.

This trend gained strength following the 2008–2009 financial crisis and has continued ever since. Community banks and regional banks were constrained by regulatory rules and often were unable to provide services to customers, notably small business loans. This was aggravated by the failure of many smaller community banks, and also by others with excessive bad loans still on their books.

Weak Loan Demand

Regional bank management was optimistic in 2018 about demand for consumer loans. By 2019, the outlook had changed. Even with lower taxes and higher spending in credit and debit card sectors, the 2018 acceleration in demand did not last. By early 2019, the overall picture was dim.

In some respects, regional banks have an advantage over larger institutions in the borrowing trends. Those larger institutions are finding low interest rates to yield equally low profit margins. But regional banks are better suited for that market, thanks to a focused customer base (geographically) and lower overall overhead. The lending activity grants regional banks a significant advantage. The CEO of Bancorp, the largest regional bank in the US, noted in late 2018 that currently it takes four days, on average, to complete a loan: "Through automation, we want to be able to do that in four minutes."[11]

Ability to Invest in New Technology

Banks used to focus on deposits as the primary test of success. In the near future, focus will shift to new technologies, notably among regional banks where competition is fierce and capitalization is limited.

Robotics and AI improve efficiency by doing away with the most labor-intensive processes, including preparation of reports for management and regulatory compliance. Regional banks cannot afford to *not* invest in technology as they see declines in deposits year over year. Whereas regional banks are seeing deposit declines, many of the larger banks are seeing increases.

---

11 https://www.pymnts.com/news/alternative-financial-services/2018/regional-banks-commercial-student-lending-loan-growth-rates/

Improved efficiency is the goal, but the question on the minds of many in the industry is whether investment in technology will make banks more efficient. Skepticism about how effective these changes comes not only from the outside, but also from inside the regional banking industry. One analyst explained that regional bank managers "believe that some of this can set them apart—just allowing them to be quicker to deliver. But my personal opinion is a lot of this stuff is just pay to play —it's stuff that you have to have. There's no direct revenue attachment."[12]

Lack of Staff in Key Growth Areas

The lack of certainty about growth is broad, but one focus should be on whether qualified staffing is available. Growth, especially into digital processes, requires experienced employees and, equally important, training of current employees to proficiently enact the new processes.

The combination of new compliance rules, rapid digital expansion, and competition, make this a top priority. Only 11% of senior banking executives expect improvement in their organizations' financial performance in the coming year. Even so, regional banks often are playing defense, focusing on regulatory compliance and reporting standards—but are not always able to meet growth in two areas: recruiting and retaining talent, and developing customer-facing technology.[13]

12 https://www.americanbanker.com/opinion/regional-banks-are-spending-heavily-on-tech-is-it-enough

13 https://thefinancialbrand.com/65210/banking-customer-technology-growth-investment-trends/

Chapter 2
Overview of Banking

Before we set forth the reasons why traditional retail banks are facing extinction, readers must understand the historical underpinnings influencing the evolution of the banking system, and the extent to which these factors give insight into the current structure and organization of banks. The past provides lessons for the present and guidance for the future. Although it is not possible to predict the future, it is possible, with a perspicacious eye, to discern the complex interaction of historical forces and factors producing favorable conditions. These have enabled a select few people to identify niches for their banks and to set the finance industry on a new and *previously unimagined trajectory*.

Brief History of Banking

Today's banking system is the latest in a long evolution of financial services. The earliest known practices of banking as attested to by written standards originated in Babylonia around the second millennium BC. These standards were in part formal laws, enshrined in the Code of Hammurabi, and transactions were apparently similar to the practices of modern-day banking. However, in that ancient agrarian society deposits were not of capital but of grain or other crops, cattle, and precious metals.

The fundamental concepts underlying the modern-day banking system were evident in these primitive arrangements. Loans were advanced, deposits were received, and borrowers paid interest. Similar rudimentary banking arrangements were prevalent in ancient Egypt, having originated in the need for grain to be stocked in warehouses of the centralized state. Depositors used written orders for taking out specific quantities of deposited grains. This system proved so effective that it became self-sustaining, spawning parallel banking practices with respect to precious metals and coinage.

The well-documented history of banking in Italy traces back to the medieval cities of Venice, Florence, and Genoa. The Medici family establishing banking practices as early as 1397, and theirs became the largest and most powerful bank in all of Europe. These banks were lenders and importers/exporters. Italian bankers within this system advanced credit to princes to sponsor their lavish lifestyles, fund wars, and assist merchants engaged in international trade. In fact, trading families at the time established most these early banks in Italy as divisions of their more wide-ranging business practices.[1]

---

[1] https://www.raabcollection.com/foreign-figures-autographs/baroncelli-rucellai-renaissance

https://doi.org/10.1515/9781547401598-002

The Peruzzi and Bardi families were the wealthiest bankers in Florence before the Medici family. As part of an imaginative vision to expand their operations, they established bank branches in various regions across Western Europe. Both family banks extended substantial loans to the King of England, Edward III, to sponsor his hundred-year battle against France, but the king ultimately fell into arrears with payments and defaulted, which contributed to the early demise of these banking giants. By 1345, both family banking enterprises had crashed.[2]

After this, the Medici Bank took control and became the most well known of the Italian banks in this period. Giovanni Medici, the bank's founder, was an astute businessman and early on shifted the business from its green-covered counter in the Florence market to a nearby palace. This move resulted in a substantial increase in wealthy clientele. Giovanni, like the Peruzzi and Bardi families, realized that to increase his banking business he needed to expand beyond Italian territorial boundaries. He established many bank branches throughout Europe, although his primary focus was on England. Due to his entrepreneurial drive, the bank quickly grew, deriving prestige both from its association with royals and merchants, and from its status as the main bank of the Papacy. Over time it was the patronage by the Popes, as compared with business derived from other clients, that resulted in gains for the bank, and this success enabled Medici to expand and establish a substantial number of bank branches.

Later, during the 17th and 18th centuries, the British and Dutch began to pattern their banking practices on the Italian medieval model. In their subsequent adaptation of this system, they incorporated new features and enhancements, one of which is attributable to the goldsmiths of London around this period: the acceptance of *fractional reserve banking*. This is a system by which commercial banks set up reserves equal to only a fraction of deposits on hand. Reserves were held as currency or precious metals, enabling banks to act as intermediaries between savers and borrowers, while maintaining liquidity for themselves and for customers.[3]

By the middle of the 17th century, the English Civil War had culminated in the termination of the goldsmiths' conventional trade of making objects from silver and gold. Hapless goldsmiths were thus compelled to create another way in which to survive, and they did this by devising means for safely storing valuable metals. Goldsmiths began accepting precious metal deposits for security purposes, and in exchange they would issue receipts. Initially, these receipts circulated as an alternative currency; however, the goldsmiths soon became aware that the depositors were not all at the same time demanding the return of their silver and gold. The goldsmiths quickly realized that they could create extra revenue streams by

2 https://thefinancialengineer.org/2013/03/31/14th-century-the-crash-of-peruzzi-and-the-bardi-family-in-1345/

3 Abel, Andrew & Bernanke, Ben (2005). *Macroeconomics* (5th ed.). New York: Pearson, pp. 522–532.

increasing the number of receipts issued as compared with the value of the metal. Accordingly, the goldsmiths promptly abandoned their prevailing mode of operation and switched to a new pattern of trading, which was to become known as fractional banking in its earliest form.[4]

Soon after, contemporaneously with the foundation of the United States in the 18th century, this banking method was introduced to the New World, leading to the integration of national and state banks into the mainstream of the United States economy. Just five years after the Declaration of Independence, the first chartered bank, Bank of North America, became operational in Philadelphia in 1781, and was the original central bank for the new country. By 1794, seventeen more bank branches had been established throughout the country.[5]

At the time, bank charters could be granted only by statute. However, by 1838 the State of New York had introduced legislation providing for the deregulation of banking and permitting any person to set up a bank, subject to the fulfillment of specific requirements. As free banking spread rapidly to other states, serious flaws became apparent in the system. For example, banks functioning under state laws enjoyed the right to issue their own bank notes, leading to the problem of currency multiplicity.

Such practice of unilaterally issuing notes was abolished following the introduction of Civil War legislation in the form of the National Banking Act of 1863, which both inaugurated a completely new system of national banks and created a uniform national currency. Additionally, this legislation continued the empowerment of state-owned banks to issue notes, but at the same time authorized the government to impose a 10% tax on state bank bills, forcing most state banks to convert to national banks. A radical innovation in banking regulation that emerged around this time was the requirement that national banks secure their notes with Treasury securities, creating a form of a bank deposit guarantee scheme. What was so revolutionary about this regulatory reform was that in the event of default by the bank, it would provide a safety net for the possessor of currency notes.

This reform came through the National Bank Act of 1863, made necessary by the expense of the Civil War and the lack of means to fund ever-higher war costs. Senator John Sherman and Treasury Secretary Salmon Chase promoted the new bill, which passed the Senate by a narrow 23–21 vote. Under terms of the act, newly formed banks were required to purchase U.S. government bonds. Ultimately, this government control over the industry led to creation of the Federal Reserve system in 1913.[6]

---

4 https://www.frbatlanta.org/education/classroom-economist/fractional-reserve-banking/economists-perspective-transcript
5 Lewis, Lawrence, Jr. (1882). *A History of the Bank of North America, the First Bank Chartered in the United States*. Philadelphia PA: J. B. Lippincott & Co. pp. 28, 35.
6 https://www.encyclopedia.com/history/encyclopedias-almanacs-transcripts-and-maps/national-bank-act-1863

The passage of the 1863 legislation was a milestone in banking regulation. Not only did it make all banks liable to comply with a single set of laws and policies, but it also established an agency called the Office of the Comptroller of the Currency, which became the precursor to the Federal Reserve System and subsequent supervisory authority over all banks.

Banking in the Modern Era

The first decade of the 20th century saw an immense banking panic in the United States. In 1907 there were numerous runs on the banks, which became known as the Bankers' Panic. The lesson was not learned. Later during the financial crash of 1929 preceding the Great Depression, margin requirements were set at only 10%. In other words, brokerage firms could lend $9 for every $1 an investor had deposited with them. When the market collapsed, brokers called in these loans, which could not be repaid. Many banks failed as debtors defaulted on debt and depositors attempted to withdraw their deposits en masse, triggering numerous bank runs. At the time, government guarantees and Federal Reserve banking regulations to prevent such panics were ineffective. Bank failures led to the loss of billions of dollars in assets, and outstanding debts during this period became even larger due to higher prices and declining incomes, estimated as high as 50%. After the panic of 1929 and during the first ten months of 1930, a record 744 banks failed in the US, and there were more than 4,000 failures by the end of the year. In 1929, there were 25,568 banks in the US, so 1930 failures represented about 16% of the previous year's totals.[7]

By April 1933, around $7 billion in deposits had been frozen in failed banks or those left unlicensed after the March Bank Holiday. This $7 billion is equivalent to $134 billion in 2019 dollars.[8]

The *March Bank Holiday* was the suspension of all banking transactions for a full week to address the banking crisis arising from bank failures and depositor runs on the banks. It was enacted through President Franklin Roosevelt's Proclamation 2039, ordering the suspension to take effect immediately. By March 9, the emergency had been reduced enough to begin reopening banks, and Congress passed the Emergency Banking Act. Under this act, the Federal Reserve became "in effect guarantors of the deposits of reopened banks."[9]

These steps did some good, but did not solve the larger problem. Bank failures continued to snowball as desperate bankers called in loans that borrowers could not repay. With future profits at risk, capital investment and construction slowed,

---

7 http://www.sjsu.edu/faculty/watkins/depmon.htm
8 https://www.dollartimes.com/inflation/inflation.php?amount=7&year=1933
9 Meltzer, Allan H. (2003). *A History of the Federal Reserve. Volume 1, 1913–1951*. Chicago: University of Chicago Press, 2003, p. 423.

and in some cases completely ceased. In the face of bad loans and worsening prospects, the surviving banks became even more conservative in their lending. Banks built up their capital reserves and made fewer loans, which intensified deflationary pressure, and a vicious cycle developed, accelerating this process. Once the proverbial dust had settled, in all over 9,000 US banks failed during the 1930s. In response, many other countries, having seen what had just happened to the United States financial system, decided to significantly increase their financial regulation. The American government at the time also decided to follow suit by establishing the Securities and Exchange Commission in 1933, and later passed the Glass–Steagall Act, which separated investment banking and commercial banking. The motivation behind this was to prevent more risky investment banking activities from causing future commercial bank failures.

During the post–World War II period and with the introduction of the Bretton Woods system in 1944, two organizations were created: The International Monetary Fund and the World Bank.[10] Encouraged by these institutions, commercial banks started lending to sovereign states in the developing world. This was around the same time that inflation started to rise in the West. The abandonment of the gold standard in 1971 surprised a number of banks whose balance sheets nosedived, and many other banks filed for bankruptcy due to developing country debt defaults. This period also marked ever-increasing use of technology in retail banking. In 1959, banks agreed on a standard for machine-readable characters (MICR) that was patented in the United States for use with checks, and which subsequently led to the first automated reader-sorter machines. In the 1960s, the first automated teller machines (ATM)/cash machines were developed, and these became more prevalent by the end of the decade. Banks during this period realized the potential use of technology, and many became heavy investors in computer technology. The banks' intention through this investment was to be able to automate much of their processing, which led to the decline of clerical staff members in banks. By the 1970s the first payment systems began evolving, eventually leading to electronic systems for both international and domestic payments. The international SWIFT payment network was established in 1973, and not long after that alternative payment processing systems began being developed by international banks encouraged by their respective governments.

Global banking and capital market services proliferated during the 1980s after the deregulation of financial markets in many countries. The 1986 Big Bang in London allowed banks to access capital markets in new ways, which soon led to significant changes in the way banks operated and accessed capital, as well as a new trend of retail banks beginning to acquire investment banks.

---

10 https://www.imf.org/en/About/Factsheets/Sheets/2016/07/27/15/31/IMF-World-Bank

Big Bang referred to the sudden decision to deregulate financial markets on October 27, 1986, led by British Prime Minister Margaret Thatcher. The London Stock Exchange went to electronic trading in place of open outcry.[11]

Banking services continued to grow throughout the 1990s largely due to a greater increase in demand from companies, governments, and financial institutions, leading to buoyant and overall bullish markets. During this 20-year period, interest rates in the United States declined from about 15% for two-year US Treasury notes to about 5%, and financial assets grew rapidly, at approximately twice the rate of the world economy. This era also saw a significant internationalization of financial markets, and the increase in US foreign investments from Japan not only provided funds to corporations in the United States, it also helped finance the federal government. The dominance of US financial markets had been waning, and because of this there was an ever-increasing interest in foreign stocks. The extraordinary growth of foreign financial markets at the time resulted from large increases in the pool of savings in foreign countries, notably Japan, and the deregulation of foreign financial markets. This led to American corporations and banks seeking investment opportunities abroad, prompting the development in the United States of mutual funds specializing in trading on foreign stock markets. Such growing internationalization and opportunities in financial services completely changed the competitive landscape, as now many banks demonstrated a preference for the universal banking model prevalent in Europe. The reason for this preference was that international banks were free to engage in all types of financial services, making it possible to engage in a variety of investments, and enabling a bank to become a one-stop supplier of both retail and wholesale financial services. The provisions affecting savings and loans were not amended until 2010.[12]

The early 2000s were largely marked by the consolidation of existing banks, and the entrance into the market of other financial intermediaries: nonbank financial institutions. Large Fortune 500 companies at the time began to realize the vast potential returns they could generate through banking, and many of them decided to find their way into the financial service community, offering unprecedented competition to established banks. Many of these nonbank financial institutions, such as American Express, J.P. Morgan Chase, and Citicorp, offered services that included insurance, pensions, mutual funds, money market accounts, loans, and credits, plus securities. By the end of 2017, revenue of the world's 15 largest financial services providers included five nonbanks: Berkshire Hathaway, AXA, Allianz, Fannie Mae, and Generali Group.[13]

This development can be traced back several years. It became a catalyst for financial innovation advancing significantly in the first decade of the 21st century,

---

11 "Big Bang 20 years on." London: *Centre for Policy Studies*. October 2006, at https://www.cps.org.uk/files/reports/original/111028101637-20061019EconomyBigBang20YearsOn.pdf.
12 https://www.law.cornell.edu/uscode/text/12/1467a
13 https://en.wikipedia.org/wiki/List_of_largest_financial_services_companies_by_revenue

and consequently further increasing the importance and profitability of nonbank finance. Most established retail banks during this period witnessed a massive decline in their profitability due to the emergence of the nonbanking industry. This prompted the Office of the Comptroller of the Currency, an independent bureau within the United States Department of the Treasury, to encourage banks to explore other financial instruments to diversify their business as well as improve their liquidity. However, as these financial instruments were increasingly reviewed and subsequently adopted by both the banking and nonbanking industries, the distinction between these two different types of financial institutions gradually started to vanish.

The culmination of financial innovations in banking over the past decade has triggered a major shift away from traditional banking to a new digital banking model. Nonbanks during this period had assistance with this change from a major catalyst, which was the evolution of personal computers and later smartphones. This technological advancement ultimately led to the right environment being created for financial transformation to gain rapid momentum in a short period.

Select Major International Events in Banking History

1100	Knights Templar run earliest known European-wide/Mideast banking until the 14th century.
1397	The Medici Bank of Florence is established in Italy and operates until 1494.
1542	The Great Debasement, the English Crown's policy, initiated coinage debasement during the reigns of Henry VIII and Edward VI.
1553	The first joint-stock company, the Company of Merchant Adventurers to New Lands, was chartered in London.
1602	The Amsterdam Stock Exchange was established by the Dutch East India Company to deal in its printed stocks and bonds.
1609	The Amsterdamsche Wisselbank (Amsterdam Exchange Bank) was founded.
1656	The first European bank to use banknotes opened in Sweden for private clients. In 1668 the institution converted to a public bank.
1690s	The Massachusetts Bay Colony became the first of the Thirteen Colonies to issue permanently circulating banknotes.
1694	The Bank of England was founded to supply money to the English king.
1695	The Parliament of Scotland created the Bank of Scotland.
1716	John Law established the Banque Générale in France, a private bank.

1717	Master of the Royal Mint, Sir Isaac Newton established bimetallism with a new mint ratio between silver and gold that had the effect of driving silver out of circulation, thus putting Britain on the gold standard.
1720	The South Sea Bubble[14] and John Law's Mississippi Bubble[15] failure caused a European financial crisis and forced many bankers out of business.
1775	The first building society, Ketley's Building Society, was established in Birmingham, England.
1782	The Bank of North America was opened.
1791	The First Bank of the United States was chartered by the United States Congress for 20 years.
1800	The Rothschild family established European-wide banking.
1800	Napoleon Bonaparte established the Bank of France on January 18, 1800.
1811	The United States Senate tied on a vote to renew the charter of the First Bank of the United States. Vice President George Clinton at the time decided to break the tie and vote against renewal, and thus the bank was dissolved.
1816	The Second Bank of the United States was chartered for five years after the First Bank of the United States lost its charter. This charter was also for 20 years. The bank was created to finance the country in the aftermath of the War of 1812.
1817	The New York Stock Exchange Board was established.
1818	The first savings bank of Paris was established.
1862	To finance the American Civil War, the federal government under President Abraham Lincoln issued legal tender paper money, called *greenbacks*.
1874	The Specie Payment Resumption Act was passed, providing for the redemption of United States paper currency in gold, beginning in 1879.

---

14 The South Sea Company was founded in 1711 as a combined private/public partnership, intended to lower the national debt. Speculators caused a sharp rise in stock price by 1720, but prices then tumbled and speculators lost all their money: https://www.amazon.com/s?k=south+sea+company&hvadid=78546414047844&hvbmt=be&hvdev=c&hvqmt=e&tag=mh0b-20&ref=pd_sl_8t6xcew7yc_e.

15 The Mississippi Bubble was a financial scheme engineered by John Law, an adventurer and economic theorist. He gained exclusive rights to develop French territories in the Mississippi River Valley. Wild speculation drove up share prices and led to a Europe-wide stock boom. The French government took advantage of this by printing paper money to be used by creditors to buy more shares. This caused extreme inflation, and the expected profits in the scheme did not materialize. By 1720, the excessive speculation caused stock prices to fall and a widespread market crash followed: http://www.thebubblebubble.com/mississippi-bubble/.

1913   The Federal Reserve Act created the Federal Reserve system, the central banking system of the United States, and granted it the legal authority to issue legal tender.

1930–33 In the wake of the Wall Street Crash of 1929, more than 9,000 banks closed, resulting in a third of the money supply in the United States being wiped out.

1933   Executive Order 6102 signed by United States President Franklin D. Roosevelt forbade ownership of gold coin, gold bullion, and gold certificates by US citizens beyond a certain amount, effectively ending the convertibility of US dollars into gold.

1971   The Nixon Shock was a series of economic measures taken by United States President Richard Nixon that cancelled the direct convertibility of the US dollar to gold by foreign nations. This essentially ended the existing Bretton Woods system of international financial exchange.

1986   The *Big Bang*, the deregulation and reform of financial markets in the City of London, served as a catalyst to reaffirm London's position as a global center of world banking.

2007   In the late 2000s the financial crisis became a credit crunch, which led to the failure and bail-out of many the world's biggest banks.

2008   Washington Mutual collapsed, the largest bank failure in history up until that point.

Chapter 3
An Imperfect System: Financial Crises

The term *financial crisis* is applied broadly to a variety of situations in which some financial assets suddenly lose a large part of their nominal value. In the 19th and early 20th centuries, many financial crises were associated with banking panics, and recessions coincided with these panics. Other situations often called financial crises include stock market crashes and the bursting of financial bubbles, as well as currency crises and sovereign defaults. Financial crises often directly result in a loss of paper wealth, but do not necessarily cause changes to the real economy.

The Financial Crisis of 2007–2009

This crisis, also known as the *global financial crisis*, is considered by many economists to have been the worst financial crisis since the Great Depression of the 1930s. It threatened the collapse of large banks and financial institutions that were considered too big to fail. For a period, many national governments were slow to act on bailing out their respective banks, which consequently led to major stock market drops around the world. One of the most affected areas was the United States, where the housing market suffered a great blow, resulting in evictions, foreclosures, and prolonged unemployment.

The financial crisis played a significant role in the failure of key businesses, major declines in financial customers' wealth estimated to be in the trillions of US dollars, and a downturn in economic activity leading to a severe recession. It also contributed to the European sovereign-debt crisis. The active phase of the crisis, which manifested as a liquidity crisis, can be dated from August 9, 2007, when BNP Paribas terminated withdrawals from its three hedge funds, citing a complete evaporation of liquidity. Then the bursting of the United States housing bubble, which had peaked in 2004, caused the values of securities tied to US real estate to plummet in price, damaging financial institutions globally. The financial crisis did not come about due to just one event, but was triggered by several:

- A complex interchange of policies that encouraged home ownership
- Easier access to loans for subprime borrowers
- Overvaluation of bundled subprime mortgages based on the theory that housing prices would continue to escalate
- Questionable trading practices on behalf of both buyers and sellers
- Compensation structures that prioritized short-term deal flow over long-term value creation
- Lack of adequate capital holdings by banks and insurance companies to back the financial commitments they were making

https://doi.org/10.1515/9781547401598-003

Questions regarding banks' solvency, the decline in credit availability, and damaged investor confidence adversely affected global stock markets, with securities suffering large losses during 2008 and early 2009. Also, economies worldwide slowed during this period as credit tightened and international trade declined. During this period, international governments and central banks responded with unprecedented fiscal stimulus, monetary policy expansion and institutional bailouts. The U.S. Congress passed the American Recovery and Reinvestment Act of 2009[1] to help kick-start the American economy. Numerous causes for the financial crisis have been suggested by financial analysts and professors, and with varying weight assigned by experts. Around this time, two scathing reports were published, and extracts from each are provided below:

- The United States Senate's Levin–Coburn Report[2] concluded that the crisis was the result of *"high risk, complex financial products; undisclosed conflicts of interest; the failure of regulators, the credit rating agencies, and the market itself to rein in the excesses of Wall Street."*
- The Financial Crisis Inquiry Commission[3] concluded that the financial crisis was avoidable and was caused by *"widespread failures in financial regulation and supervision," "dramatic failures of corporate governance and risk management at many systemically important financial institutions," "a combination of excessive borrowing, risky investments, and lack of transparency"* by financial institutions, ill preparation and inconsistent action by government that *"added to the uncertainty and panic,"* a *"systemic breakdown in accountability and ethics," "collapsing mortgage-lending standards and the mortgage securitization pipeline,"* deregulation of over-the-counter derivatives, especially credit default swaps, and *"the failures of credit rating agencies"* to correctly price risk.

A major policy event that also should be considered as contributing to the financial crisis was the 1999 repeal of the Glass-Steagall Act,[4] which effectively removed the separation between investment banks and depository banks in the United States. Many critics continue to argue that credit rating agencies and investors failed to accurately price the risk involved with mortgage-related financial products, and that governments did not adjust their regulatory practices to address 21st-century financial markets. Criticism pointed out that governments had not commissioned the undertaking of in-depth research into the causes of the various financial crises that had occurred before, which could have helped prevent the 2007–2009 crisis from

1 https://www.congress.gov/bill/111th-congress/house-bill/1/text
2 https://www.hsgac.senate.gov/imo/media/doc/PSI%20REPORT%20-%20Wall%20Street%20&%20the%20Financial%20Crisis-Anatomy%20of%20a%20Financial%20Collapse%20(FINAL%205-10-11).pdf
3 https://cybercemetery.unt.edu/archive/fcic/20110310172443/http://fcic.gov/
4 https://www.cato.org/publications/policy-analysis/repeal-glass-steagall-act-myth-reality

happening. In the immediate aftermath of the financial crisis, palliative monetary and fiscal policies were adopted to lessen the shock to the economy, and the Dodd–Frank regulatory reforms[5] were enacted in the United States to reduce the chance of a recurrence. Additionally, the Basel III[6] capital and liquidity standards became more widely adopted by most countries around the world, which helped stabilize markets.

Financial Innovation and Complexity

Although much is known about the 2007–2009 financial crisis and its causes, surprisingly less known is how financial innovations and their complexity played a significant part in creating the largest global financial crisis since the Great Depression. The term *financial innovation* refers to the ongoing development of financial products designed to achieve particular client objectives, for example: offsetting a particular risk exposure such as the default of a borrower or assisting with obtaining financing. Examples pertinent to this crisis include the adjustable-rate mortgage, the bundling of subprime mortgages into *mortgage-backed securities* (MBS), or *collateralized debt obligations* (CDO) for sale to investors (a type of securitization), as well as a form of credit insurance called *credit default swaps* (CDS). The use of these products expanded dramatically in the years leading up to the crisis. All these products vary in complexity due to the ease with which they can be valued on the books of financial institutions. To illustrate the sheer growth of some of these financial innovations, CDO issuance grew from an estimated $20 billion in Q1 2004 to its peak of over $180 billion by Q1 2007, but then declined back under $20 billion by Q1 2008.

CDOs are promissory vehicles to pay investors in a specific order based on cash flow collected from a pool of bonds and other debts. Repayment is made depending on the seniority of investors and, in the event of insufficient profits, junior investors would not be paid in full.[7]

Although it must be stated in conjunction that the credit quality of CDOs declined from 2000 to 2007 as the level of subprime and other non-prime mortgage debt increased from 5 to 36% of CDO assets. Other financial innovations such as subprime lending, CDSs, and a portfolio of CDSs called a *synthetic CDO* enabled a theoretically infinite amount to be wagered on the finite value of housing loans

---

5 https://www.cftc.gov/LawRegulation/DoddFrankAct/index.htm
6 Basel III is a series of international regulations to promote stability in the international banking and financial system. It reformed international banking regulations that became apparent after the 2007 subprime crisis: https://www.bis.org/bcbs/basel3.htm.
7 McLean, Bethany & Nocera, Joe (2010). *All the Devils Are Here, the Hidden History of the Financial Crisis*, New York: Penguin, p. 120.

outstanding, provided that the buyers and sellers of these derivatives could be found. For example, buying a CDS to insure a CDO ended up giving the sellers the same risk as if they owned the CDO, when those CDOs became worthless. This happened because many issuers of CDOs failed to follow their own guidelines and added low-quality debts to pools in addition to the higher-quality instruments described as part of the product. Once returns began declining and defaults set in, many pools—including those promising to limit holdings to high-quality debts—failed, and the result was losses in the millions of dollars.

This major boom of innovative financial products went hand-in-hand with the development of the ever-increasing complexity of these innovations. For example, the multiplication of the number of people and companies connected to a single mortgage, including mortgage brokers, specialized originators, the securitizers and their due diligence firms, managing agents and trading desks, and finally investors, insurers, and providers of repo funding. With increasing distance from the underlying asset, these connected businesses started relying more and more on indirect information, including FICO scores on creditworthiness, appraisals and due diligence checks by third-party organizations, and what they considered most important: the computer models of rating agencies and risk management desks. Instead of this spreading risk, it instead provided fertile ground for fraudulent acts, mismanagement, and finally market collapse. This collapse was a direct consequence of issuers selling worthless securities as part of what were supposed to be high-quality investment pools. The problem for investors was believing they could trust the issuers; and the problem for the issuers was failure to regulate their own practices.

Martin Wolf summarized the situation when he wrote in June 2009 that certain financial innovations enabled firms to circumvent regulations, such as off-balance sheet financing that affects the leverage or capital cushion reported by major banks, stating: *"... an enormous part of what banks did in the early part of this decade—the off-balance-sheet vehicles, the derivatives and the 'shadow banking system' itself—was to find a way round regulation."*[8]

Regulatory Overhaul

The severity of the financial crisis necessitated a massive public expenditure, so that various international governments could bail out certain banks that were about to fail, provoking a populous chorus of "Never again!" Since the banking regulation, supervision, and corporate governance had failed in numerous countries, it reinforced the commonly held view that banking crises are recurring phenomena. After the 2007–2009 financial crisis, however, a substantial number of people

---

8 Wolf, Martin (June 23, 2009). "Reform of regulation has to start by altering incentives." FT.com.

requested that a review be undertaken of banking regulation and supervision across the globe. The regulations drafted in response to this public outcry were primarily aimed at addressing bank liquidity, capital, corporate structure, and compensation. The hope for these policy initiatives was that they would lead to a stable international financial system for many years to come.

These wide-ranging regulatory reforms for the international banking sector constitute one of the most turbulent periods of regulatory transformation in contemporary history, exemplified by the enactment of more than 80 substantial pieces of legislation and rules after the crisis.

These global banking reforms included a diverse array of policies plus specific measures, and select examples of some of the banking/financial laws enacted after the crisis include the following:

- **Banking: Conduct of Business Sourcebook (BCOBS)** — Insists that banks are fair, clear, and not misleading in their communication with customers. The Financial Conduct Authority (FCA) can now fine banks or even in some cases remove them from the register if they infringe on these rules.[9]
- **Extension of the FSA's Approved Person Regime** — Extends a regime ensuring bankers are "fit and proper." Competency, honesty, and integrity are all considered in their assessment.[10]
- **FSA Remuneration Code** — Makes pay more transparent, discourages short-term risk-taking, and allows for the return or repayment of bonuses.[11]
- **Banking Act of 2009** — Allows the Bank of England to close a bank before its balance sheet becomes insolvent, to keep the financial system stable.[12]
- **European Market Infrastructure Regulation (EMIR)** — Introduces new requirements to improve transparency and reduce the risks associated with the derivatives market. This simplifies clearing requirements for smaller firms and simplifies the threshold calculations, removes frontloading requirements for derivatives trading, and amends reporting requirements.[13]
- **Capital Requirement Directives (CRD II & CRD III)** — Makes banks safer by requiring them to hold more capital and improve their management of liquidity risk. This enables firms to meet less stringent requirements as long as they do not deal in their own accounts or underwrite financial instruments.[14]

---

9 https://www.handbook.fca.org.uk/handbook/BCOBS.pdf
10 https://www.amazon.com/s/?ie=UTF8&keywords=fsa+approved&tag=mh0b-20&index=aps&h vadid=78683853869722&hvqmt=p&hvbmt=bp&hvdev=c&ref=pd_sl_10p8xhnlhc_p
11 https://www.fca.org.uk/firms/remuneration
12 http://www.legislation.gov.uk/ukpga/2009/1/pdfs/ukpga_20090001_en.pdf
13 https://www.nortonrosefulbright.com/en/knowledge/publications/e78883ef/ten-things-you-need-to-know-about-the-emir-review
14 https://www.fca.org.uk/firms/crd-iv/remaining-crd-iii

- **CRD IV** — Implements internationally agreed standards on "more capital, more liquidity" across the European Union, making it easier for banks to facilitate international trade and provide additional forbearance for customers in mortgage arrears, as well as introducing a cap on remuneration to members of firms and mortgage originators.[15]
- **Banking Reform Act of 2013** — Implements a framework for compartmentalizing the largest banks to better protect customers' deposits, legislates for bail-in measures to ensure that taxpayers' money will not be used to save failed banks, introduces a Senior Manager Regime to hold key decision-makers accountable, and makes severe misconduct a criminal act. Following the 2008 financial crisis, regulators reviewed how risk oversight operated and improved standards of conduct among senior management.[16]
- **Bank Recovery and Resolution Directive (BRRD)** — Requires banks to prepare recovery plans and authorities to be ready to resolve failed banks without recourse to the taxpayer while requiring creditors to be "bailed-in."[17]
- **Single Resolution Mechanism (SRM)** — Complements the Single Supervisory Mechanism (SSM) and provides a structure within which to coordinate the resolution of a failed bank, including the possibility of creating a Single Resolution Fund.[18]
- **Deposit Guarantee Schemes Directive** (DGSD) — Enhances protection for bank account holders by increasing the coverage and transparency of their deposit guarantee.[19]
- **MAR/CSMAD** — These two pieces of legislation together extend the scope of the current market abuse regime to cover financial instruments traded on new categories of platforms and the OTC. This affects anyone who conducts insider deals, improper disclosure, misuse or manipulation of insider information, or who conducts business based on insider information. The revised regulations expand civil penalties to include criminal penalties as well for some forms of insider dealing. This will more closely align the way in which market abuse rules apply to commodity derivative and underlying spot markets, which include improper activities relating to benchmarks within the scope of market manipulation, introducing offenses of attempted insider dealing and market

---

15 https://www.regulationtomorrow.com/eu/remuneration-in-crd-iv-firms/
16 http://www.allenovery.com/publications/en-gb/lrrfs/uk/Pages/The-Banking-Reform-Act-2013.aspx
17 https://financialmarketstoolkit.cliffordchance.com/en/topic-guides/bank-recovery-and-resolution-directive-brrd.html
18 https://srb.europa.eu/en/content/single-resolution-mechanism-srm
19 https://ec.europa.eu/info/business-economy-euro/banking-and-finance/financial-supervision-and-risk-management/managing-risks-banks-and-financial-institutions/deposit-guarantee-schemes_en

manipulation, ensuring national competent authorities have a minimum set of investigative and enforcement powers, and establishing a harmonized regime of minimum criminal and administrative sanctions across all of the EU Members States.[20]

- **Markets in Financial Instruments Directives (MiFID II/MiFIR)** — Improves investor protection, increases transparency, and continues the harmonization of regulation across the EU.[21]
- **EC Bank Accounts Legislative Package** — Increases access to basic banks accounts, improves transparency, and legislates to make account switching easier.[22]
- **Packaged Retail Investment and Insurance-Based Products (PRIIPS)** — Increases the consistency and transparency of complex investment and insurance products for retail customers.[23]
- **Central Securities Depositories Regulation** (CSDR) — Harmonizes securities settlement in the European Union.[24]
- **Multilateral Interchange Fees (MIF) Regulation** — Reinforces the *single market* (meaning the European Union) by promoting more secure, innovative, efficient, and competitive card payments.[25]
- **Fair and Effective Markets Review** — Raises standards, professionalism, and accountability of individuals and strengthens regulation of fixed Income, currency, and commodities markets. This is accomplished with a wholesale review of how the markets operate, in order to identify and correct root causes leading to past misconduct.[26]

A New Potential Role for Banks

Despite the reputational damage retail banks suffered from the financial crisis, they still hold a trusted position in society as the stewards of assets and commerce. While the public still does give low ratings to the banking industry on matters of trust, their opinions about the banks they do business with are far more favorable.

---

20 https://www.financierworldwide.com/the-csmad-significant-imminent-changes-to-eu-market-abuse-and-insider-dealing-rules#.XKika5hKi70

21 http://solutions.refinitiv.com/mifid?utm_content=MiFID%20II-US-AMER-Phrase&utm_medium=cpc&utm_source=bing&utm_campaign=68832_RefinitivBAUPaidSearch&elqCampaignId=5917&utm_term=mifid&msclkid=4eab1b8288d5164fd357472a2d884e00

22 https://ec.europa.eu/info/law/law-topic/eu-banking-and-financial-services-law_en

23 https://www.investopedia.com/terms/p/packaged-retail-investment-and-insurancebased-products-priips.asp

24 http://www.dtcc.com/regulatory-compliance/csdr

25 http://emoneyadvice.com/mif-ifr/

26 https://www.fca.org.uk/news/speeches/fair-and-effective-markets-review

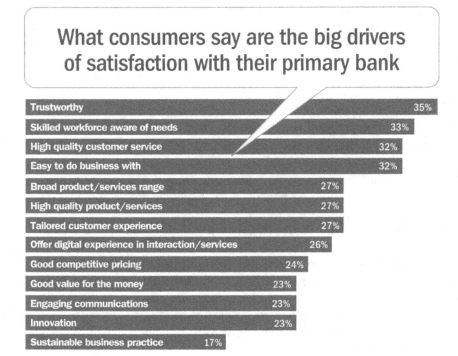

What consumers say are the big drivers of satisfaction with their primary bank

Driver	Percentage
Trustworthy	35%
Skilled workforce aware of needs	33%
High quality customer service	32%
Easy to do business with	32%
Broad product/services range	27%
High quality product/services	27%
Tailored customer experience	27%
Offer digital experience in interaction/services	26%
Good competitive pricing	24%
Good value for the money	23%
Engaging communications	23%
Innovation	23%
Sustainable business practice	17%

Figure 3.1: What consumers say are the big drivers of satisfaction with their primary bank. Source: Accenture © July 2015. The Financial Brand.

This is a critical advantage in the digital era, because when it comes to handling personal data, customers always trust their bank above any other provider. Banks that can use client data to deliver value to them without sharing it with others are the most favored of all. This now puts banks in a potentially advantageous position, due to new analytics technologies making it possible for banks to use transaction data to deliver savings to customers as well as generate revenue for themselves. For those financial consumers who are satisfied with their trusted relationship (see Figure 3.1), this now presents banks with a new frontier for loyalty and growth. However, banks must not lose focus on earning the right to a deeper commercial relationship by maintaining transparency and inviting their customers to "opt in" by choosing further benefits, rather than banks deciding this for them.

Chapter 4
Rapid Transformation

The global economic crisis from several years ago has ushered in a new era for financial services, largely due to the emphasis on the still extreme inefficiency of the existing banking system. The picture is emerging due partly to expanding online banking services.

The Customer Shift

To the extent that customers use online banking, boundaries are obscured and no longer matter. For those relying on physical bank branches, regional banking can be substantially different in rural Nebraska or central Manhattan—let alone in Africa, South and Central America, the Middle East, or in many Asian countries where bank branches are rare or difficult to get to.

This emerging change in how people bank has contributed to banks entering a period of unprecedented disruption, in part because financial service innovations have contributed to a completely new way in which customers can bank, through the increased mass adoption of mobile technology to the digitization of cash. These changes have threatened the competitiveness of traditional retail banks and are redefining a banking model that had been unchanged for decades. Established banks are being forced to increase their pace of digital adoption, as well as drastically reduce their overheads through cost-cutting measures such as reducing the number of bank branches in which they operate (see Figure 4.1).

Modern financial consumers want a simple experience, using bank products that are easy to understand and that are transparent and accessible 24/7. A distinction must be made between basic services customers receive and services they want. All customers expect four basic services: transaction management, lending, savings, and financial guidance. What customers want today is a less tangible list of benefits, and simplicity in keeping track of their money is at the top of this list. Banks that make it easy tend to create customer loyalty. Bankers have always thought that offering more services and opening more branches were the keys to success. However, customers want to be able to keep their complex money matters simple and close at hand. This does not mean offering services that only a few people want, but it does mean being able to address concerns.

This is precisely what fintech companies as nonbank providers are delivering and is a reason why so many consumers are adopting fintech solutions in record numbers (see Figure 4.2). Financial technology companies are fast becoming recognized as the innovation engine for the banking industry, and retail banks were caught unaware, perhaps even failing to know how to respond. Banks have had

https://doi.org/10.1515/9781547401598-004

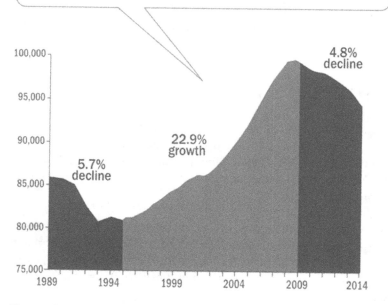

Figure 4.1: Total number of bank branches in the United States (1989–2014).
Source: The Federal Deposit Insurance Corporation © February 2015. The Financial Brand.

time to understand the situation, but many seem to not know what the emerging customer base means to their survival. Banks now have a significant amount of catching up to do. For these established banks to stay relevant, they need to act quickly and should be continually scanning the market for fintech companies to emulate, partner with, or acquire. With many banks operating like financial disruptors, obsessing about customer experience and utilizing the latest in digital technology to stay competitive are only part of the picture.

Fintech Overview

Financial technology, or *fintech*, is an industry composed of companies that use technology to make financial services more efficient. Fintech companies are generally start-ups trying to disrupt incumbent banking systems, with the aim of challenging those traditional corporations that are less reliant on technology. Also, note that

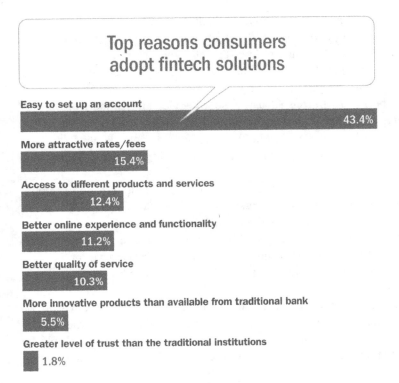

Figure 4.2: Top reasons consumers adopt fintech solutions.
Source: Ernst & Young © December 2015. The Financial Brand.

fintech can also apply to any financial innovation that people use to transact business, and since the advent of the mobile revolution, this sector has grown explosively. A recently released report by Accenture estimated that global investment in financial technology has increased more than twelvefold, from $930 million in 2008 to more than $12 billion in 2014, and the industry has been earmarked by many industry analysts for rapid growth over the next five to ten years. For banks, *growth* usually means acquisition of smaller regional banks. This is the "easy" way, but more focus on responding to customer preferences may create long-term growth.[1]

To demonstrate the impact fintech has on our lives, it's been reported that 40% of the city of London's workforce is employed just in financial and technology services. Some of these respective companies include Funding Circle, Nutmeg, and TransferWise with all three firms currently experiencing unprecedented success.

---

[1] https://newsroom.accenture.com/archive.cfm

In the US there are many similar companies, including Affirm,[2] Betterment (a top start-up of 2018),[3] Behalf (in Technology "Fast 50" for 2016),[4] Fundera,[5] IEX (winner of Benzinga Fintech Award),[6] Lending Club (fintech blog),[7] Money.net (platform for analysis and comparison),[8] Nomis Solutions (aimed at helping banks win customer engagement),[9] Plaid (developer of banking access tools),[10] Prosper (fintech blog),[11] Robinhood (on the *Forbes* fintech 50 list),[12] SoFi (service and support provider),[13] Square (developer of the easy-payment system),[14] Stripe (developer of online fintech infrastructure services),[15] and Wealthfront (for building free financial plans).[16]

These companies and many more like them are thriving in the rapidly expanding fintech world.

An EY Global study in 2017 showed that 50% of the adopters were for money transfers and payments; insurance was next with 24%, followed by savings and investments at 20% and then borrowing and financial planning at 10% each.[17]

Studies have estimated that at least $8 billion was invested in financial technology companies in 2018, an increase from $3.5 billion only five years earlier.[18]

The five most significant and expanding fintech hubs today are in Sydney, Australia; London; China; New York; and South Africa.[19]

World-class fintech companies with leading online platforms include WeLab (offering one of China's largest mobile lending platforms),[20] which raised the second-largest Series B fundraising in fintech globally.[21] Another company to watch out for in the region is VMoney from the Philippines. The company has a proprietary online

---

2 https://www.affirm.com/press/releases/affirm-unveils-updated-brand-new-logo-and-shopping-features-in-time-for-the-holidays/
3 https://www.betterment.com/press/newsroom/the-fintech-250-the-top-fintech-startups-of-2018/
4 https://www.behalf.com/about/
5 https://www.fundera.com/about
6 https://benzingafintechawards.com/vote-2018/iex/
7 https://thefintechblog.com/tag/lending-club/
8 https://internationalfintech.com/Company/money-net/
9 https://www.lendit.com/usa/2018/sponsors/nomis
10 https://plaid.com/company
11 https://thefintechblog.com/tag/prosper/
12 https://www.forbes.com/companies/robinhood/#4f03b3446076
13 https://www.sofi.com/our-story/
14 https://thefintechblog.com/tag/square/
15 https://stripe.com/about
16 https://www.wealthfront.com/
17 https://www.ey.com/en_gl/banking-capital-markets/four-themes-driving-fintech-adoption-by-consumers
18 https://www.statista.com/statistics/412056/global-investment-in-fintech-companies/
19 https://channels.theinnovationenterprise.com/articles/where-are-the-fintech-hubs
20 https://www.welab.co/en
21 https://www.welab.co/en/press-release/welab-series-b

platform, which enables members to deposit money into digital wallets where it can then be sent to other VMoney members in real time, transferred to bank accounts, or used to pay bills or reload a prepaid card. The company offers all its members a pre-paid MasterCard that can be used for both online and point-of-sale transactions.[22]

Not to be outdone, the academic community has also played a substantial part in the growth of fintech through research and the creation of industry organizations. One such established group is the Financial Data Science Association (FDSA),[23] which was founded by members from the artificial intelligence, machine learning, and natural language processing domain, with the aim of building a research community around computer science and investment statistics.

A noteworthy university initiative is Wharton's FinTech,[24] which was founded at the Wharton School, of the University of Pennsylvania, in October 2014. The main aim of the organization is to connect academics, innovators, investors, and other thought leaders within the industry to each other, to discuss and foster ideas that could reinvent global financial services.

Another significant contribution by academia includes the University of Hong Kong's Faculty of Law in conjunction with the University of New South Wales – Faculty of Law,[25] which published the research paper "The Evolution of Fintech: A New Post-Crisis Paradigm?"[26] The purpose of this research was to trace back the history of fintech and look at how the regulation overseeing the industry has evolved since its inception.

Fintech Outlook

Fintech's future appears to be exceptionally positive, due to constant innovation among financial start-ups and share growth of the financial market through reduction of shares held by global retail banks. The number of financial customers who will change over to fintech in the coming years will continue to increase because of a growing technological savvy that seeks companies that offer the latest in financial innovations and lower-cost options to conduct financial services.

Bumps in the road should be expected due to enforcement of the Bank Secrecy Act (BSA),[27] and money transmission regulations represent an ongoing threat to fintech companies (see Figure 4.3). In addition, some analysts have commented that although fintech companies are the disruptors, they themselves could be vulnerable to

---

22 http://fintechnews.sg/26724/philippines/e-wallets-in-the-philippines/

23 https://fdata.global/

24 https://www.whartonfintech.org/

25 https://www.law.hku.hk/faculty/index.php

26 https://papers.ssrn.com/sol3/papers.cfm?abstract_id=2676553

27 https://occ.treas.gov/topics/compliance-bsa/bsa/index-bsa.html

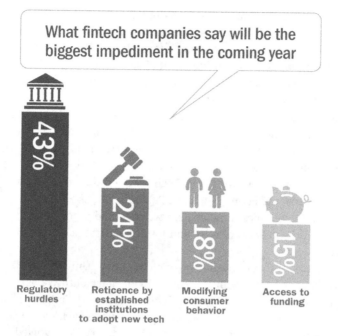

Figure 4.3: What fintech companies say will be the biggest impediment in the coming year. Source: Silicon Valley Bank © November 2015. The Financial Brand.

disruption through software. This is because financial services, much like publishing, is made up of information rather than tangible goods, and companies can be made obsolete virtually overnight if a better version of the software or service they provide is released by a competitor. Closely aligned with this is concern with the issue of trust. Customers must have trust in their banking relationships, and will move if that trust is compromised.

A 2018 study on digital transformation by EY Global paints a slightly different, but complimentary picture, citing lack of properly skilled teams as the first obstacle, integrating new and existing tech as the second and inflexible or slow processes as the third significant barrier.

Chapter 5
The Financial Disruptors

New fintech entrants are moving rapidly into traditional areas of banking as they expand their customer base. Examples of companies making these moves include Google, offering a debit card to go with its mobile wallet service; telecommunications providers T-Mobile in the US, Rogers in Canada, Airtel in India, and SingTel in Singapore, all of which have rolled out similar mobile wallet services; and Walmart and American Express, which attracted over one million customers with Bluebird, a pre-paid card offering a low-cost alternative to checking account services in the United States.

Platforms such as Apple's iPhone already provide seamless and secure mobile financial services to hundreds of millions of customers though Apple Pay. Though many of the new entrants lack the scale to pose an immediate threat to traditional retail banks, these changes could come swiftly due to the continued increase in technological advancements. Many established retail banks are waking up to the impending threat that technology companies pose. One retail bank survey indicated this growing concern (see Figure 5.1).

It hasn't just been the larger players influencing the industry. Smaller and medium-sized disruptive financial start-ups are also experiencing success and rapid growth. One such example is Square, a point-of-sale payment-processing venture that has accumulated over 7 million monthly users (as of December, 2018).[1] Whether large or small, the already mentioned fintech companies have contributed enormously to the development of new innovative technologies within the global financial industry, all of which has laid the groundwork for major disruption and the current retail banking revolution.

PayPal

PayPal Holdings, Inc., considered the world's largest online payment company, was established with the purpose of creating the first payment-based system to adapt to internet e-commerce. The company's services allow people worldwide to make financial transactions on the internet by granting the ability to transfer funds electronically between individuals and businesses. Through PayPal's leading technology platform, users can send or receive payments for purchases, online auctions, or even sell goods and services, donate money, or receive donations. PayPal's users can also use the company's services to send funds to anyone with an email

---

[1] https://www.pymnts.com/mobile-applications/2018/square-cashed-in-7m-users-for-cash-app/

https://doi.org/10.1515/9781547401598-005

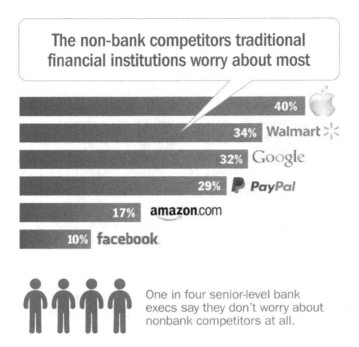

The non-bank competitors traditional financial institutions worry about most

- 40% Apple
- 34% Walmart
- 32% Google
- 29% PayPal
- 17% amazon.com
- 10% facebook

One in four senior-level bank execs say they don't worry about nonbank competitors at all.

Figure 5.1: The nonbank competitors traditional financial institutions worry about most. Source: Bank Director © September 2015. The Financial Brand.

address. To receive these funds, it's quite a simple process, and all the recipient needs to have is a registered PayPal account associated with that same email address. A basic PayPal account is free, as are most of the financial transactions that can be initiated through PayPal's website, at least domestically; overseas transactions may be subject to fees.[2]

One of the key reasons for PayPal's overwhelming success to date is that the company provides people with a better way to manage and move their money, offering them choice and flexibility in how they can send money, pay, or get paid. In 2016 the company reported that it operates in 203 markets and has 179 million active, registered accounts allowing customers to send, receive, and hold funds in 26 different currencies worldwide.

PayPal is headquartered in San Jose, California, and the company is licensed as a money transmitter in order to be able to carry out its various services within the US as well as internationally. Ask any payment industry professional, and they will tell you that PayPal is without a doubt the biggest financial digital disruptor of all

---

2 https://www.paypal.com/

time. Future expectations are that the company will continue to be a pioneer and lead the development of new fintech innovations well into the future.

Square

Square, Inc. is primarily a financial services company, as well as a merchant aggregator and mobile payment operator, based in San Francisco, California. The company markets several of its software systems and hardware payments products, which include the Square Register and Square Reader. The company has also now expanded into small business services such as Square Capital, a financing program, and Square Payroll. What makes it unique is the business model, in that the company decided to provide its magnetic stripe card readers to its users for free. The Square app is also freely downloadable from Apple's App Store and Google Play Store. The company generates revenue by charging a fee of 2.75% on every credit card transaction. It does not charge users any additional fees beyond this swipe, nor any monthly fees or initial setup costs.

Square is widely regarded as having one of the most user-friendly phone apps available for entrepreneurs. It allows people to offer their clients the ability to use a debit or credit card via smartphone, with none of the major costs normally associated with retail point-of-sale system machines. Swiped payments are then deposited directly into a user's bank account, and are generally available within one or two business days. The company also generates revenue from selling other services to businesses, including subscription-based products such as Customer Engagement, Square Payroll, and Square Register. A notable major development for the company came in mid-2015 when Apple announced that Square would release a new Square Reader capable of accepting Apple Pay and other contactless payments, and that the reader would accept EMV chip cards as well. By 2019, the chip card was well established, boasting the ability by Square to process chip cards in two seconds.[3]

Square has become synonymous with mobile payments and has done what no one else had managed to do so before: make credit card payments accessible to everyone. One of the principal reasons for the company's success to date is that its product is exceptionally easy to use, thus making commerce simple for anyone. Another key to success is how Square designed its mobile app to work on almost any mobile device. The Square interface also receives praise for its simplicity and elegance, and it's no wonder the company has incredible name recognition even with the multitude of new competitors it now faces. As of 2019, analysts following

---

[3] https://www.pymnts.com/news/payment-methods/2018/square-emv-transactions-chip-cards-mobile-payments/

Square estimate, on average, annual growth of 25%, based on recent growth in earnings of over 600% (2018 over 2017).[4]

Square is expected to continue to successfully expand its customer base, while at the same time creating new business lines and maintaining its strong core payment business. Although Square's focus to date has been small to mid-sized businesses, it's thought that the company will increasingly push to work with bigger companies, which will more than likely yield higher fees, as well as boost the company's profits.

Amazon

Amazon is the world's largest online retailer, by total sales and by its market capitalization. The company sells categories of goods ranging from electronics and books to jewelry, groceries, and auto parts. It's considered the most innovative online retailer, due to having developed its own propriety e-commerce technology platform. One part of the company's strategy is that it employs a multi-level e-commerce approach, which originally started by focusing on business-to-customer (B2C) relationships between itself and its customers, and then business-to-business (B2B) relationships between itself and its suppliers. Now Amazon has made the move to incorporate customer-to-business (C2B) transactions as it understands the value of customer reviews as part of product descriptions. The company also facilitates customer-to-customer (C2C) interactions with the provision of the Amazon marketplace, which acts as an intermediary to assist with C2C transactions.

The retailer truly does enable almost anyone to sell almost anything using its platform. Its much-celebrated affiliate program lets anybody post Amazon links and earn a commission on click-through sales, and another program lets those affiliates build entire websites based on Amazon's platform. By leveraging and expanding its self-developed technology, Amazon could therefore develop many different web services. An example of this is Amazon Web Services (AWS), a subsidiary of Amazon.com, which offers a suite of cloud-computing services that make up an on-demand computing platform. These services operate from 60 Availability Zones across the world.[5] The best known of these services is arguably the Amazon Elastic Compute Cloud, or EC2, and the Amazon Simple Storage Service, or S3. AWS offers dozens of services, spanning a wide range, and this expands every month. These services include computing, storage, networking, database, analytics,

---

4 https://www.nasdaq.com/symbol/sq/earnings-growth
5 https://www.allthingsdistributed.com/2018/12/introducing-the-aws-stockholm-region.html

application services, web app deployment, API management, and mobile and developer tools.[6]

There is no question that the marketplace of the future will be a digital-driven world, a combination of electronic selection and payment with high-speed physical delivery systems over a broad range of goods and services. In this marketplace, Amazon sees its customers not as part of a casual trade walking in off the street, but rather as members of a club to which they have great loyalty. At present the company is still developing its future customer experience, and many believe that the company is defining, not chasing, future customers and will be profitable long into the foreseeable future.

Facebook

Facebook is an online social networking service based in Menlo Park, California. Its network allows people using mobile phones or computers to stay in touch with relatives, friends and other acquaintances wherever they are in the world. Users can share or broadcast content to others in order to share their feelings and points of view. In the wake of digital transformation, Facebook has achieved significant success in encouraging people to enter this new digitalized world. Recently reported data by Facebook indicated that it had 2.23 billion monthly active uses as of September, 2018 with forecasts showing that users will continue to increase.[7] The company made its first public offering in 2012 and started to sell stock to the public three months later, achieving an original market capitalization peak of more than $104 billion. By mid-2015, Facebook was already the fastest-growing company in the S&P 500 Index, attaining a market cap of more than $250 billion, and only a few months later the market cap continuing to soar to well over $300 billion. By the beginning of 2019, Facebook's market cap was $501.50 billion.[8]

In 2015 the company announced one of its most innovative features for its Messenger service, which lets users send and receive money to one another. Users who add their debit card information within Messenger's settings can then send payments by starting a conversation with a friend, selecting the $ icon that appears, and then just selecting Pay. Users who receive money do so by opening that respective friend's message and accepting the payment when prompted. Both sides of these transactions are user-friendly and represent a remarkably convenient way to make payments.

Facebook has now moved well beyond its early identity as a social networking site for younger people. It's now the indisputable world leader in the social

---

6 https://aws.amazon.com/ec2/
7 https://www.omnicoreagency.com/facebook-statistics/
8 https://ycharts.com/companies/FB/market_cap

networking market, with a total user base of 2.41 billion in the second quarter of 2019 despite only 3 million in 2018 in China.[9]

Facebook's global impact will continue to grow, as 26% of the world population uses Facebook,[10] and more than 44% of the world's 7.75 billion people have yet to come online.[11] The company has also benefited from the mobile revolution, and has 1.04 billion mobile daily active users as of early 2019.[12] The company has been exceptionally innovative in turning this mobile trend into monetization through Facebook mobile ad sales. In 2018 this service represented 93% of total advertising revenue, a 61% annual gain as of 2018.[13] As of April, 2019, the consensus forecast among 47 polled investment analysts covering Facebook was 70% "buy" recommendations.[14]

Google

Google, LLC, a subsidiary of Alphabet, Inc., is a multinational technology company based in Mountain View, California, specializing in various Internet-related products and services. Much of Google's earnings are derived from AdWords, an online advertising service enabling people and companies (see Figure 5.2) to advertise on a search results page. Google's fast growth since incorporation has enabled the company to make many acquisitions, partnerships, and products beyond its core activity as a search engine provider. Additional non-core services include online productivity software such as Google Drive for cloud storage service and Gmail.

The company has long been considered a trailblazer in financial technology, and is at the forefront of the mobile payments scene with Google Wallet enabling online payments and money transfers since 2011. In 2015 Google joined forces with Amazon, Apple, Intuit, and PayPal to form Financial Innovation Now,[15] with the aim of promoting policies to foster technological innovation in the financial services space. Google's ethos is that financial services technology is on the brink of change, and that fintech entrepreneurs need to be ready to ride this new digital wave.

One of the company's flagship products, Google Wallet, is a peer-to-peer payments service created to allow people to send and receive money from a mobile device or computer at no cost to either sender or receiver. Once set up, a Google

---

9 https://www.statista.com/statistics/558221/number-of-facebook-users-in-china/
10 https://internetworldstats.com/facebook.htm
11 https://internetworldstats.com/stats.htm
12 https://thenextweb.com/facebook/2016/01/27/90-of-facebooks-daily-and-monthly-active-users-access-it-via-mobile/
13 https://www.mobilemarketer.com/news/facebooks-2018-ad-revenue-surges-38-to-55b-amid-stories-ad-growth/547286/
14 https://www.marketwatch.com/investing/stock/fb/analystestimates
15 https://financialinnovationnow.org/

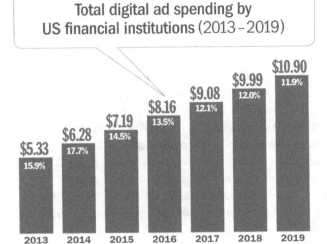

Figure 5.2: Total digital ad spending by US financial institutions (2013–2019).
Source: eMarketer © May 2015. The Financial Brand.

Wallet account must be linked to an existing debit card or bank account. The service can be used through Gmail, with a downloadable app available for Android devices. However, there are limits on the amounts of money users can add to their Wallet balance, withdraw from their linked accounts or cards, or send and receive to other individuals.

Since inception, Google has developed a wide range of products and services that have captured customer needs and reshaped customer expectations regarding how they can communicate, make payments, and source information. The rapid growth and expansion of Google demonstrates not only how the company is a key player in digital transformation innovation, but in how it can also rightly be called one of the most important financial disruptors of the last decade.

Skrill

Skrill[16] is an e-commerce business allowing payments and money transfers online, with a core focus on offering low-cost international money transfers. The company is based in London, UK, and is registered as a Money Service Business with Her

---

16 https://www.skrill.com/en-us/

Majesty's Revenue and Customs. Skrill is regulated by the Financial Conduct Authority (FCA)[17] and licensed to operate anywhere within the EU.

The company allows sending and receiving payments of in 41 currencies, as well as providing support for a variety of credit and debit cards on its platform. Skrill accounts can be held in any one of the major currencies, but there is a limitation: once the first transaction is made it is not possible to change the account's currency.

Individuals can open an account with Skrill through registering an email address and entering personal data via the company's website. Users can complete an optional identity verification process, which allows sending and receiving of higher-value payments. Accounts are identified by one or more email addresses associated with them, and payments from a Skrill account (other than withdrawals to one's own bank account or a payment card) are processed by sending money to an email address.

An email address assigned to a Skrill account can only be altered or removed with the help of Skrill support, and accounts are limited to four email addresses. Customers of the company also can purchase a Skrill-branded prepaid card, linked to their account, in any one of four major currencies: USD, EUR, PLN (the Polish Złoty), and GBP.

High-turnover customers are offered premium membership called Skrill VIP that includes additional features, such as a security token, multi-currency accounts, and earning loyalty points. For businesses, Skrill offers a payment gateway as well as escrow payments, assisting companies with international trade while mitigating risk on critical transactions.

Skrill is one of Europe's largest online payments systems and is among the world's largest independent digital wallet providers, with over 36 million account holders, and this all bodes well for Skrill to continue its success long-term.[18]

TransferWise

TransferWise[19] is a peer-to-peer money transfer service launched in January 2011 and headquartered in London with offices in Tallinn and New York. About $4 billion of users' money is transferred per month through the company for 4 million customers.[20]

The creation of TransferWise was inspired by the personal experiences of the company's founders, who as Estonians working between their native country and the United Kingdom had personal experience of the pain of international money transfers due to high bank charges on amounts they needed to convert from Euros to

---

17 https://www.fca.org.uk/
18 https://www.skrill.com/en-us/siteinformation/about-us/
19 https://transferwise.com/us
20 https://transferwise.com/us/about/our-story

British Pounds and vice versa. This sparked the idea of setting up a private arrangement, with payment in Euros placed directly into a payee's Estonian account so that the recipient could pay bills without having to convert between currencies.

The recipient pays via British pounds. This led to development of a crowd-sourced currency exchange service, offering a cheaper alternative to established retail banks, and in February 2012 TransferWise received approval from the Financial Conduct Authority in the UK to commence operations. After its first year of operations the company founders knew that they potentially had a very successful business when transactions through TransferWise amounted to almost $12 million at a time when it was still relative unknown.

From the customer's point of view, money transfers using TransferWise are not that different from other conventional money transfer services, with the customer choosing a recipient, a currency, and an amount. The money is transferred, taken from the user's account for a nominal fee, and the recipient receives payment. However, the difference with TransferWise is in how it routes the payment. Instead of transferring the sender's money directly to the recipient, it is redirected and an equivalent transfer goes in the opposite direction, which then is paid to the recipient. This process enables the user to not be charged with a costly currency conversion, typical of international transfers via retail banks.

The key to the company's success is the prevailing attitude of financial customers in today's marketplace. Everyone has had enough of retail banks charging exorbitant fees to facilitate international transfers. The TransferWise digital strategy is an easy-to-use product and not meant to make the owners of the company or product wealthy. To date, the company's service has been popular with Millennials, who are the key drivers for digital services such as this. TransferWise aspires to one day become the company that the majority of international businesses use for their payments in order to reduce their banking costs. In 2015 TransferWise received funding of $58 million in its Series C funding round, led by US venture capital firm Andreessen Horowitz. The company also has an impressive list of initial backers including Sir Richard Branson, Peter Thiel's Valar Ventures, Index Ventures, IA Ventures. and Seedcamp.

Alibaba

In late 2012 Amazon made headlines when it announced the creation of Amazon Lending, a service providing loans to merchants selling through the company's web platform. At the time, this seemed revolutionary for a major e-commerce provider, but Amazon was actually following in the footsteps of Alibaba,[21] the online e-commerce giant that established the same idea three years earlier in China.

---

21 https://www.alibabagroup.com/en/global/home

Users of Alibaba.com, China's dominant e-commerce website, employ a variety of services, especially Alipay,[22] which controls more than 82% of China's online payment market. The speed in which Alibaba has grown offers a salutary warning to retail banks, due to the company gaining an increasingly larger foothold in the Chinese banking market. In only four years Alibaba became the world's largest online payments provider and has parlayed this into other ventures, such as providing commercial lending by using data about its small business members to assess their creditworthiness. This led to growing Alibaba's loan book to $16 billion in only three years.

One of Alibaba's most extraordinary achievements is found in its financial affiliate, Ant Financial Services Group. This is the world's fourth-largest money market fund. Alibaba gained such large footholds within the financial industry in such a short space of time primarily through offering clients deposit interest rates of up to 15 times higher than standard savings rates in China. This enabled Alibaba to attract the equivalent of 20% of all new Chinese deposits within only nine months of its launch. The company has outlined ambitious plans for growing its market share, and announced plans to offer new wealth management advisory services, as well going live with a new credit card service. By 2019, this effort was well under way. Alibaba also plans to pursue additional growth in the next five years not only through the creation of new services, but via targeted acquisitions, such as owning one-third of Ant Financial.[23]

Facing mass-market erosion, many of Alibaba's competitors have urged regulators to treat funds such as the Alibaba money market as ordinary deposit accounts, which would require Alibaba to set aside 20% of its holdings as reserves. Chinese regulators have increasingly cited the need for supervision of online funds, but have consistently restated the importance in bringing financial innovation to the region. As of the end of fiscal 2018, sales and earnings exceeded industry expectations, and estimates are that the company will outperform in coming years as well:[24]

Fiscal Year	In millions of Yuan	
	Revenue	Earnings
2015	76,204	24,320
2016	101,243	71,289
2017	158,273	41,226
2018	250,266	61,412

---

22 https://intl.alipay.com/
23 https://www.paymentsjournal.com/keeping-an-eye-on-alibaba-ant-financial-and-alipay/
24 https://www.statista.com/statistics/298844/net-income-alibaba/

Cryptocurrencies

Bitcoin[25] is a digital asset and payment system, operating peer-to-peer, enabling direct transactions between users without the need for an intermediary. These financial transactions are verified by network nodes and recorded in a public distributed ledger called the *blockchain*, which uses bitcoin as its unit of account.

Because the system works without a central repository or single administrator, the US Treasury categorizes bitcoin as a decentralized virtual currency. Bitcoin is often referred to as the first *cryptocurrency*, although prior systems did exist, so it is more correctly described as the first decentralized digital currency. In 2019, Bitcoin was the largest of its kind in terms of total market capitalization, at $91.6 billion.[26]

Bitcoin value is created as a reward for payment processing work. Users offer computing abilities to verify and record payments into a public ledger. This is called *mining*, and miners are rewarded with transaction fees and newly created Bitcoins. Besides being obtained by mining, Bitcoins can be exchanged for other currencies, products, and services. When sending Bitcoins, users are given a choice to pay an optional transaction fee to the miners.[27]

Bitcoin has been the most successful cryptocurrency to date, because instead of the 2–3% typically imposed by credit card processors, merchants accepting Bitcoins pay fees that range from zero to less than 1%. The significant increase in the number of Bitcoin users has recently gained traction with retail transactions. As of 2019, 32 million users are identified; and 7.1 million active Bitcoin users do not even include the number of emerging users and markets.[28]

Currently the legal status of Bitcoin varies substantially from country to country, and is still undefined or changing in many of them. Whereas some countries have explicitly allowed its use and trade, others have either completely banned or severely restricted its use. However, more than 200 countries allow commerce based on Bitcoin and other cryptocurrencies.[29]

Bitcoin is only 10 years old as of 2019, and it may take many more years for its infrastructure to be established. Many people advocate for the cryptocurrency claiming they can imagine its true potential, although realistically they need to think in terms decades, not in months or years.

Other cryptocurrencies are in wide use beyond Bitcoin. Ethereum[30] is second only to Bitcoin in popularity, and many say it has faster transaction speed.

---

25 https://bitcoin.org/en/
26 https://coinmarketcap.com/
27 https://www.ibtimes.co.uk/bitcoin-now-accepted-by-100000-merchants-worldwide-1486613
28 https://www.bitcoinmarketjournal.com/how-many-people-use-bitcoin/
29 https://www.investopedia.com/articles/forex/041515/countries-where-bitcoin-legal-illegal.asp
30 https://www.ethereum.org/

Ripple[31] is most efficient when transactions take place between countries and currencies. Litecoin[32] has competitive transactions fees of 35 cents (as of late 2018). Zerocash (Zcash)[33] was the original coder for Bitcoin. However, unlike Bitcoin, all transactions on Zcash are anonymous. Bitcoin's market value per share was impressive in 2017, when it rose from under just under $1000 to just under $20,000.

Stellar[34] uses remittance companies and credits, simplifying transactions between countries. Nem[35] allows users to make transactions publicly or privately, and commercial adaptation is facilitated by the use of integrated blockchain technology. Iota[36] is designed to work best with IoT (internet of things) devices; it may become the cryptocurrency of choice as IoT technology expands.

Monero[37] is set up for *anonymous transacting*, which may gain in popularity in the future as a growing number of users resist public trading in cryptocurrencies. Finally, Cardano[38] is efficient for transacting digital funds and also is used as a platform for creating new decentralized apps. A large number of developers are attracted to this site, though its valuation in early 2019 is extremely low.

Given the range of features and special applications, the selection of one cryptocurrency over another depends on your personal preferences and needs. This is a new field that continues to expand rapidly every year.

Other Applications of the Blockchain

Cryptocurrency, distributed ledger, and blockchain technology are much more than an alternate form of currency. The digital revolution in distributed ledger technologies includes development of *smart contracts*. These are "contracts" between buyer and seller or parties wishing to perform a transaction that are written in lines of code. The contract is spread across a decentralized network of the blockchain, allowing agreements to be entered between anonymous parties. There is no need for a legal system, external enforcement, or authority to approve or enforce the contract.

This is one way in which cryptocurrency and its blockchain technology is evolving in the digital revolution. The idea of anonymous contracts in digital form is

---

31 https://ripple.com/
32 https://litecoin.org/
33 https://z.cash/
34 https://www.stellar.org/
35 https://nem.io/
36 https://www.iota.org/
37 https://www.getmonero.org/
38 https://www.cardano.org/en/home/

revolutionary and raises many questions. In traditional contract law, one long-standing principle is identification of the parties to the contract. With a smart contract, this is not necessary.

What are the applications of this idea? Imagine that you enter an agreement with a casualty insurance company and later have an accident. In the traditional manner, you have to put in a claim, and an adjuster views the damage and authorizes a payment. With a smart contract, that entire process could be automated and as soon as you put in a claim, an electronic payment is made to the body shop of your choice. Of course, many questions arise regarding fraud and trust, dollar value of damages, and control by the insurer over levels of claims received and approved.

The concept is being tried through systems like Open Law, which is developing standard contracts commonly in use but without needing an attorney or other expert. Part of the smart contract idea is to develop legally enforceable code as part of the blockchain itself. This has its complexities, but the first steps have been taken, and the future will determine the extent of applications that would be suited to this technology.

Criticism has also been offered. A 2019 *Forbes* article, "Blockchain Smart Contracts Aren't Smart and Aren't Contracts," made the point that these agreements have many security issues. Users have to understand that a smart contract is an immutable software program that offers a stored procedure that will carry out the terms identified in the software. If it is incorrectly set up, it is irreversible. It might be a clever idea, but in practice it does not meet the legal definitions of a *contract*—known parties reaching a meeting of the minds, with offer and acceptance and performance carefully spelled out. Lacking these elements, what happens if one side breaks the agreement? How does the digital world enforce the terms (if, in fact, the terms were spelled out)?

Even though smart contracts are an exciting idea, the concept needs to be tested and proven before it can replace the well-known legal document. For example, most people will agree that a written contract is preferable to a verbal contract. Is the smart contract either one? Or, as the article in *Forbes* asked, is it even a contract?

Indeed, the best applications of blockchains may be carrying out transactions in a manner that automates processes that do not allow for exception. Smart contracts need not be contracts in the current sense of the word today, but they likely will be in the future. In any event, it is clear that this technology, or modifications of it, will offer huge benefits. Applications other than cybercurrencies are in use and in development today, and tasks that require intervention, especially expensive intervention, are certainly candidates for this solution.

Chapter 6
The Digital Financial Revolution

The rapid transformation of financial services is truly remarkable. Only five years ago, most people had never heard of *fintech*, let alone used a fintech company to make in-store payments or international money transfers. The industry expectation is that over the next several years, gradually more people will begin to trust fintech providers for their financial service needs. The more established banking is in a region, the less impact change brought on by fintech will have. For instance, in China financial offerings at banks in many regions have leapfrogged those in the US, where satisfaction remains high for the current system and regulation remains stiff. Surprisingly the Millennials in the US have a quite strong affinity for trusted banking at their local neighborhood banks. So, regional differences come into play, most significantly outside the more established banking centers, and safety is a key concern that has been under-emphasized worldwide. Fintech providers must work to guarantee their customers safety in their transactions to succeed.

These factors come into play whether it's the issuance of a credit card (there are thousands of issuers, but the 10 biggest control 90% of the entire market[1]) or obtaining a mortgage, with at least 26,000 mortgage companies in the U.S.[2] As of December 18, $470 billion in outstanding balances was reported by Chase, Bank of America, American Express, Citibank, and Capital One.[3]

A trend underway is distrust among older adults, who tend to shun the use of mobile payments altogether. In early 2015, the Federal Reserve decided to ask various financial consumers in the US why they do not utilize their bank's mobile app to conduct their financial services. The chart shown in Figure 6.1 outlines the responses received.

A similar survey from the Fiserve and Harris Poll in 2018 asking why consumers don't use P2P payments yielded similar results with 49% saying they used other methods, 41% not wanting to pay a fee, 25% not knowing how it works and 21% concerned about security.

To date the most common experience of people in using a fintech company has been for payments in-store, with a large number having expressed that they had used a service such as Apple Pay or Android Pay to purchase goods in a retail shop. The next most common experience for people using a fintech company was to make international payments, followed next by obtaining a loan, and the fourth reason of use was for managing personal investments. Mobile banking trends grow every year.[4]

---

1 https://www.creditcards.com/credit-card-news/credit-card-statistics.php
2 https://thebasispoint.com/many-mortgage-loan-officers-companies-u-s-2q2017/
3 https://www.creditsoup.com/articles/2018/12/credit-card-companies/
4 https://www.valuepenguin.com/banking/statistics-and-trends

https://doi.org/10.1515/9781547401598-006

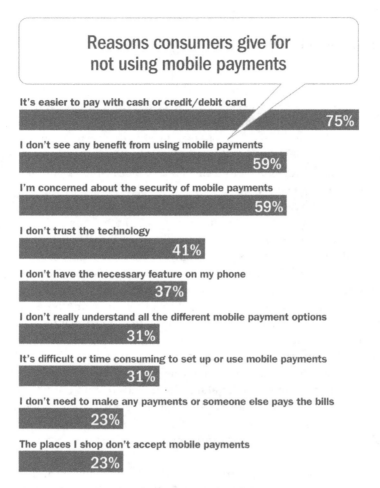

Figure 6.1: Reasons consumers give for not using mobile payments.
Source: Federal Reserve © March 2015. The Financial Brand.

Reasons given by certain financial consumers for the change have included better and more personalized experience of fintech companies, as well as the lower costs of their products and services.[5]

Digital financial service firms have been making large inroads into the banking sector over the last decade, although their success to date has been varied. Some have experienced limited growth but others, notably PayPal, have been successful. It was only when the underlying conditions discussed in the following sections changed

---

5 https://smartasset.com/checking-account/online-vs-traditional-banks-which-is-better

within a short space of time that fintech companies were finally able to rapidly emerge and gain significant market share from more established players.

Loss of Customer Trust

Banks in well-established markets have "circled the wagons" and are now racing to beat or consume the fintech competition. The global financial crisis of 2007–2009 created a seismic shift in the dynamics of trust in banking services, and thus made a slight opening for fintech companies to gain a foothold. What has further eroded consumer trust in retail banks is that in the years since the crisis, 20 of the world's biggest retail banks have paid more than \$235 billion in fines, from having breached a variety of financial regulations during and before the crisis.[6] Though that amazing statistic is not well known to typical consumers, the damage done by the financial crisis and by incidents like the Wells Fargo account scandal have left doubt in the minds of consumers.

Industry analysts have stated that banks have not regained much if any of the trust that was lost.[7] Per Edelman's Trust Barometer, financial services as an industry is ranked at the bottom in trust in 2019, below historically disliked industries such as pharmaceuticals, oil and gas, and big tobacco companies.[8]

The emergence of fintech companies would have eventually happened, but without the global financial crisis it would have taken longer for them to emerge and gain a decent share of the market. Even so, the entire industry has a long way to go to improve public perception and trust worldwide.

Better Service Experience

The disruptive innovation developed by fintech companies has provided financial customers with not only a better banking experience but—largely because of their cost structures—are providing services that are faster, cheaper, and more convenient than those of a retail bank. In addition, customers are now being provided with many alternative service offerings beyond those traditionally offered by banks. By comparison, the banking industry still has an outdated look and feel about it. Retail banks will now be forced to play catch-up, with many of them needing to

---

6 https://www.marketwatch.com/story/banks-have-been-fined-a-staggering-243-billion-since-the-financial-crisis-2018-02-20

7 https://www.americanbanker.com/opinion/banks-are-running-out-of-time-to-regain-public-trust

8 https://www.edelman.com/sites/g/files/aatuss191/files/2019-03/2019_Edelman_Trust_Barometer_Global_Report.pdf?utm_source=website&utm_medium=global_report&utm_campaign=downloads, p. 47.

overhaul their technology systems and online service offerings. Those banks making a concerted effort to improve their digital offerings will be rewarded by the ability to be competitive, and not to be rendered obsolete by the rapid rise of financial technology companies and their innovations.

The Arrival of Millennials

The rise of Millennials has ushered in a new demographic whose expectations are different from those of prior generations. They are the largest generation in the history of the US labor force[9] and will soon command the largest purchasing power as well. They spend $200 billion annually as of 2018[10] and will spend $10 trillion over their lifetimes as customers in the United States alone. Typically, Millennials do not have the same legacy relationship with their banks as older generations do. Still, 95% of Millennials in the US rated their bank as good or better. Not surprisingly, 92% said they prefer banks offering digital services.[11] In the UK, with 168 million deposit accounts, only one million customers switch a year according to a February 2018 study.

The growth of fintech has been driven by adoption across all age groups, but the concerns over demand from the Millennial generation to innovate and to think about financial services differently has been a major catalyst for the disruptive change in the finance industry.

Mass Adoption of Smartphones

As mobile device manufacturers keep releasing newer versions of their phones and operating systems, the world's leading retail banks struggle to keep up with the demand of their customers for newer more innovative digital applications (see Figure 6.2). This innovation gap poses significant risks for established financial institutions as they face increased pressure from new *digital challenger banks*,[12] a term used in the UK to describe banks directly competing with established banks.

---

9 https://www.pewresearch.org/fact-tank/2018/04/11/millennials-largest-generation-us-labor-force/

10 https://www.forbes.com/sites/julesschroeder/2017/10/31/how-to-tap-into-the-millennial-200-billion-buying-power-with-social-media/#16220e5a1161

11 https://www.workingmediagroup.com/why-millennials-are-leaving-your-bank-and-how-to-stop-them/

12 Wallace, Tim (December 29, 2015). "Are challenger banks the saviours of British banking?" *The Daily Telegraph*.

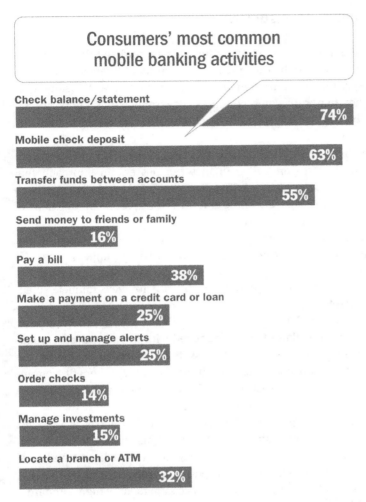

Figure 6.2: Consumers' most common mobile banking activities.
Source: Bank of America © July 2015. The Financial Brand.

A generation of digital natives may quickly lose patience when their digital needs are not met.

In many respects presently the banking sector shows an inability to innovate and catch up with society's wider trends of digital innovation. This is an alarming development, as gaps and shortcomings in retail banking and mobile apps expose a clear risk that new nimble fintech competitors will take advantage of these established players' weakness and make substantial inroads, particularly with Millennials.

Regulation for Financial Consumers

The banking industry is now regulated as tightly as ever, and rightly so because customer protection must always be the number one priority of financial regulatory authorities. However, regulation can often encourage innovation at the same time as protecting customer rights. In some countries, government regulators are approachable and flexible and have responded much faster to the advent of financial service innovators.

For example, in the UK the Financial Conduct Authority (FCA) has set up a Project Innovate to work with innovative finance businesses, an approach that other jurisdictions, such as Australia and Singapore, have followed. The approach being taken by these countries is refreshing due to the active encouragement of nonbanks to compete in financial services.

Although in other countries the process of change has been slow, with a company still required to obtain a bank license to perform a whole range of financial services, even if it restricts itself to one activity, such as payments. The result of a policy like this is that it makes it exceptionally difficult for new financial challengers to enter the market.

April 2015 saw an exciting development for the fintech industry when the new heralded Payment Systems Regulator (PSR)[13] launched with the objective of broadening access to the United Kingdom's payment systems. As more nonbanks use payment systems directly, financial customers will now be able to benefit from increased competition and better services being offered. Regional regulatory agreements, for example in the EU, can also encourage innovation.

For instance, the EU is a large internal market, with only one set of rules for payments requiring just one-member state authorization. This enables a business to "passport" into all the member states. It's no coincidence that a large number of new payment companies have been developed within Europe recently. Crucially, authorities have realized that flexibility can still be accompanied by high standards. For example, in the UK all companies must meet the standards as set out by the FCA for the services they want to provide to customers. Financial service providers must meet the same standards, as this ensures continued customer trust in the sector whether people use a traditional retail bank or a new fintech company.

More Efficient Financial Services

In the past, the only way to compete with a retail bank was to set up another bank. Now with recent technological advancements, almost any type of financial entity

---

13 https://www.psr.org.uk/

can be set up anywhere in the world. The primary reason for this is that today there is no longer a need for central control, with each problem having to be solved independently. This new way of operating has completely transformed the regulatory landscape and laid the groundwork for the first initial wave of financial disruptors to emerge. The majority of fintech companies in the sector have been remarkably strategic in how they approach the banking industry, focusing on just one aspect of the product and service offering of retail banks. In this way fintech companies may ensure better products by removing or reducing charges and dramatically improving the customer experience. Now they do not need to compete initially with all the same products and services against retail banks. Instead fintech companies can focus on one or two service areas where they can become competitive, gaining market share rapidly.

Looking to the future, many experts within the banking industry now consider that this approach by fintech companies could lead to the demise of traditional retail banks. Most traditional retail banks focus on profits in customer banking by opaquely bundling services together. Banks have also generated revenue by attracting customers through free or heavily subsidized checking accounts, and once the client is on-board, they then apply hidden charges on the bundled services, including overdraft fees and hefty cash withdrawal fees from ATM/cash machines. An extensive report published by the United Kingdom's Competition and Markets Authority (CMA)[14] in 2018 revealed that reforms in banking practices, notably in fees charged, were underway. Reforms include correction of personal current accounts that charge fees despite being advertised as free. These have been growing at alarming rates, especially for overdrafts and ATM usage.[15]

While the European Union's European Banking Authority has been aggressive in banking regulation, customers have come to expect more from nonbanks in terms of clarity than retail banks, and this along with added services can lead to significant disruption within the industry. The likely area of banking that will see these changes first is lending, particularly loans for small businesses. A case in point is the United States, where bank lending to small firms rose only 2.5% between June 2015 and June 2016, to $614 billion, with loan balances declining below 2008 levels.[16] In the EU, small business lending fell in 15 of 25 countries.[17]

This tightening of credit between 2008 and 2016 and the ratcheting up of costs made it much easier for new entrants like Funding Circle[18] and Lending Club[19] to gain

14 https://competitionandmarkets.blog.gov.uk/2018/02/06/retail-banking-remedies/
15 https://www.cnbc.com/2017/07/21/the-crazy-growth-of-bank-fees.html
16 https://www.sba.gov/advocacy/small-business-lending-united-states-2016
17 http://www.oecd.org/newsroom/small-business-access-to-alternative-finance-increasing-as-new-bank-lending-declines.htm
18 https://www.fundingcircle.com/
19 https://www.lendingclub.com/

market share almost immediately, due to financial customers over the last decade being actively on the lookout for alternatives to traditional retail banking options. Another probable area of the banking business that will see significant disruption is the facilitation of international payments and transfers. This is primarily due to the number of fintech companies that now provide a better solution at a lower cost for this type of service. Financial customers have known for some time now that they were being subjected to paying higher bank fees but felt powerless because there have been no real alternative financial services providers—until now.

Rules of Supply and Demand

Invariably new financial entrants will always find their way to a market where large numbers of people have already turned to nonbank fintech companies for their banking needs. Even those financial customers who don't currently need or use a fintech service will consider them as an alternative due to the increased presence of these companies operating in their area. In addition, will people gain trust in tech pioneers such as Google, Amazon, and Facebook? Will they trust these organizations with their personal information, and will they naturally also start to become more trusting of fintech companies? The answers are unknown as of 2019.

However, there is a common misconception that the security of nonbank providers is nowhere near the level of traditional retail banks, and this been a major barrier in the uptake of services by fintech companies (see Figure 6.3). On the other hand, several research studies undertaken in the last two years have indicated that this is not the case, and the primary barrier is simple due to a lack of awareness of fintech companies and the services they provide. To overcome this will be difficult for many new financial service firms because creating awareness and getting new customers to trust an unknown brand or service, especially those digital disruptors that lack a physical bricks and mortar presence, will prove a tough challenge. Still, the future of fintech is considered to be exceptionally positive due to retail banking trust levels being at an all-time low. Financial companies are continually becoming more prevalent, and this will likely lead to an ever-increasing number of customers who will make the change from their retail bank.

An Industry Transformed

As the existing retail banking model is being redefined, everything about the financial services experience will be changing, and within only a few years the industry will look remarkably different. A host of new financial providers and

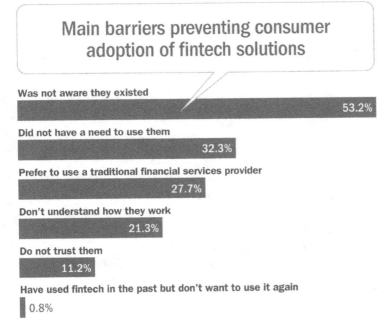

Figure 6.3: Main barriers preventing consumer adoption of fintech solutions.
Source: Ernst & Young © December 2015. The Financial Brand.

innovative new services will emerge. Some retail banks will have taken digital transformation seriously, others will buy their way into the future by acquiring challengers, and some will just be forced out of business. Certain segments of the industry will be almost entirely controlled by nonbanks, whereas other segments will be better off within the structural advantages of a retail bank. Overall, financial consumers will be the main beneficiaries of this change due to increased competition lowering costs and yielding innovative improvements to the customer service experience.

Nevertheless, the most important result of these changes will be the true democratization of the financial services industry. The current banking model is fundamentally unfair, due to the costs of using the banking system plus the profits of banks being overwhelmingly accrued from fees and charges that hit the poorest hardest (see Figure 6.4). International payments are a prime example: for a large proportion of those making these types of transfers, the transfer fee cost is a huge burden. Per a study by the World Bank, the reduction in the cost of sending international payments since 2010 has been driven by the emergence of new, cheaper alternatives, which has already saved customers approximately more than $60 billion since 2010. As fintech companies drive change and innovate, the result will be the

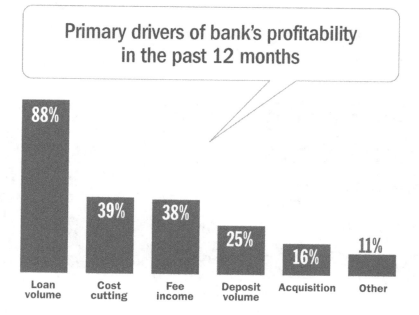

Figure 6.4: Primary drivers of banks' profitability in the past 12 months.
Source: Bank Director © September 2015. The Financial Brand.

extension of financial opportunity for many more people around the world. This will be largely because of two reasons: first, fees charged will no longer be dispro-portionate to the financial service, and savings and investments will accrue better returns.

Chapter 7
A New Era of Banking

With cash being overtaken by card payments for the first time, and enhancements in technology now at the forefront, digital banking is fast becoming the primary outlet for financial customers to properly manage their finances. It may seem counterintuitive, but technology has in fact allowed us to have a closer relationship with our bank than ever before. The average user of Barclays logs into the mobile app 28 times a month, not far off from once a day. It's difficult to imagine people visiting their local bank branch or phoning their bank at least once a day.

This change has been driven by financial customers today requiring reliable updates on their financial positions, whenever and wherever they choose. Similarly, millions of retail bank customers have signed up for and grown accustomed to receiving text messages on their phones, giving them notice if they are about to slip into the red or breach the terms of their overdraft agreements. These alerts remind many of us to transfer funds into our accounts, or alternatively to speak to our bank's customer service department to avoid being assessed fees.

The industry is changing its level of financial innovation, enabling customers to more easily find out whether they may be better off by moving their banking elsewhere. For example, the service Midata[1] allows customers from a growing number of high street banks to download a year's worth of account data, including interest accrued, any overdraft charges, and costs associated with traveling overseas. They can then upload the data to a price comparison website such as GoCompare[2] and see a ranking of which of the hundreds of current accounts on the market would provide the best value for them.

Mobile banking, check imaging, and smartwatches are just some of the latest financial innovations assisting customers with a variety of ways in which to spend, move, and manage their money. Unquestionably many more of these types of financial innovations will be created over the coming years, to try to win the hearts and minds of customers and convince them to switch accounts (see Figure 7.1). The extent of how far this innovation can be developed is still not known. The ability of digital banking firms to continue their rapid growth will ultimately be bound to the reliability of new technology advancements, and their performance will also be directly affected either positively or negatively by this.

A Forrester Research survey in August 2018 asked about the most important factors in selection of a new banking provider and the major factors were lowest fees,

---

1 https://www.midata.coop/en/home/
2 https://www.gocompare.com/

https://doi.org/10.1515/9781547401598-007

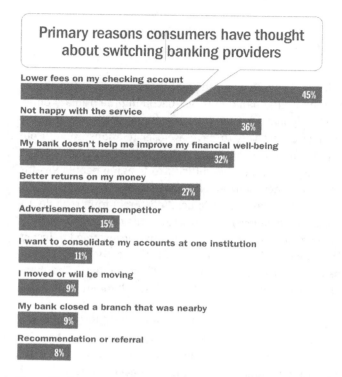

Figure 7.1: Primary reasons consumers have thought about switching banking providers. Source: Market Force © December 2015. The Financial Brand.

local branches and friend or family recommendation. Again, we see a significant difference in the survey results.[3]

Banking on the Go

The emergence of banking mobile apps has completely revolutionized the way in which financial customers can interact with their banks. Now customers can check their balances, make payments, and perform a range of other financial tasks on the go. People seem to love the convenience of being able to check their balances via a quick login process, which only takes a few seconds from wherever they happen to be at the time.

---

3 https://www.crnrstone.com/insightvault/2018/08/23/how-consumers-choose-a-bank-a-tale-of-two-surveys/

Once customers log in to their accounts, they are presented with numerous options. Client banking portals are able to facilitate almost any financial service, with virtually no difference between what you can get done with a member of your bank's staff in one of their local branches versus online by yourself. Therefore, mobile banking apps have become popular compared to the alternative—visiting your branch or calling your bank's customer service call center. Requests can more simply be achieved in the palm of your hand from wherever you are located.

Exemplifying the speed in which financial customers have been adopting mobile technology, Halifax, a division of Bank of Scotland, reported that the number of logins on its mobile banking app in the United Kingdom reached almost 40 million during March 2016, nearly double the number from March 2015. A record number of retail banks have reported that mobile banking apps have eclipsed Internet banking portal usage via browsers for the first time. This shows the swift take-up of mobile banking services is ever increasing, and so too is their sophistication. Barclays recently added an innovative feature to its mobile banking app, which now clearly displays the unsecured credit limits for its customers. This is a level of transparency that is a world away from how personal credit decisions were made in the past. Previously a bank customer would have had to travel to a bank branch and complete a detailed application process, even though his credit rating had probably already been decided in a department or division elsewhere within the bank. Barclays has reported a lot of positive feedback on its new innovative feature. By proactively making customers aware of how much they can borrow, the bank enables them to decide whether this is the right time in their lives to take on more debt.

Certain retail banks also offer a faster, more transparent loan application process online, and customers can have funds deposited into their accounts within minutes. In many instances this speed and control over personal finances isn't just useful, but can save customers a significant sum of money. For example, say you have been reviewing cars at your local dealer when you happen to stumble across a vehicle ideal for your needs. While standing there, you realize that you don't have the funds available to buy the vehicle outright. You will probably find yourself looking at the terms of a finance package offered by your local car dealer because you would not yet have had a chance to travel to your bank's nearby branch. The likelihood is that you will now be offered a rate far higher than what you would have received from your bank. With some mobile banking apps you can apply immediately to borrow money from your bank and will receive the funds a short time later, deposited directly into your account—all without leaving the car dealership. Because your bank has a clearer understanding of your risk profile, you will more likely be offered a considerably lower interest rate than if you had accepted the financial package from the car dealership.

Halifax has taken this system one step further. It now allows customers to prearrange secured financing for a car they plan to buy, and have the car loan money transferred to the dealership once the sale has been agreed. These faster, more streamlined credit application processes are proving to be increasingly more popular with customers. Barclays reports that a third of its personal loan applications received are now approved without the customer having to visit a local bank branch.

HSBC, not to be outdone, has also added new services to its mobile banking app, which now include the ability to apply for credit and the ability to open a new bank account by taking a selfie picture to verify the user's identity. Its mobile bank app uses facial recognition software to take a headshot of the customer, which is then compared against a photo identification uploaded by the customer, such as a driver's license or passport. This new method is intended to simplify and speed up the process of opening a new account using a mobile device and reflects the increasing willingness of financial customers to open personal bank accounts online.

About one-half of all credit accounts were opened online as of 2018.[4] This is compared to just 10% of accounts in 2013. Banks have adopted biometric technology to improve security. *Biometrics* include the use of facial recognition, eye print authentication, voice identification, fingerprint scans, finger vein readers, and the measuring of heart rate, to verify a customer's identity. Other financial service providers using this technology include NatWest and the Royal Bank of Scotland, use biometric checks for their credit card customers. Biometric security is becoming ever more common, due to the technology becoming cheaper and the convenience it provides financial customers.

There is still a long way to go before biometrics becomes the industry stand for authentication, but the potential benefits it offers are quite evident. A personal identification number (PIN) can be easily stolen with a quick glance over a shoulder, whereas stealing a fingerprint is far more difficult. Another newly developed app feature by HSBC allows customers to extend their overdraft facilitated through their mobile bank app, which could prove quite useful for some financial customers to manage. For example, you visited a retailer over the weekend, but it was before your payday and you saw a great deal on an appliance that you desperately needed. Not that long ago you wouldn't have had any option available for you to purchase it other than through credit cards. Now you can open your mobile bank app and extend your overdraft facility right from the store. This is a perfect example of the fast, helpful financial service innovations provide customers with unrivaled customer service experiences as compared to just a few years ago.

Contactless Cards

The traditional bank credit or debit card may not automatically spring to mind as quickly as the washing machine or the lawnmower when one thinks of great time-

---

4 https://www.creditcards.com/credit-card-news/how-we-apply-for-credit-cards.php

saving innovations, but every day people line up in shops all around the world and make purchases by swiping them. Now with *contactless* payments, customers simply tap a card reader at checkout rather than punch in a four-digit PIN or scribble a signature on a screen or receipt. These tap payments can take about a second to complete, whereas conventional chip and PIN transactions or using cash take much longer. This financial innovation saves time for retailers and customers alike. For example, Tesco, the British multinational grocery and general merchandise retailer, has measured the time taken for customer payments and estimates that contactless payments are approximately six seconds faster than card chip and PIN payments. In the first half of 2018 alone, contactless transactions jumped by 66% to 158 million payments.[5]

This swift uptake in usage can be explained by the London transport system's adoption of this innovative technology. Today, passengers traveling by tube, bus, and many overland trains in London now pay by tapping their bank cards when they begin and end their journeys. An estimated 40% of all trip payments are made by contactless transactions.[6]

This also means not having to line up at ticket offices or topping up an Oyster card online. These payments are not only faster, they are also safer than other payment methods due to three main reasons:

1. The nominal maximum limit imposed on contactless transactions in most cases is approximately USD 40—hardly a bounty for any fraudster.
2. If customers spend more than the maximum amount over a short period, they are prompted to enter a PIN, thus substantial instances of fraud are unlikely.
3. Many contactless terminals are located in places with CCTV footage, and criminals will likely think twice and realize that the risks of being caught far outweigh the rewards.

The contactless payment rollout continues in the United Kingdom, with the Department for Transport aiming to introduce this technology across all of Britain's buses, trains, and other modes of public transportation. This payment method has proven so popular that the government had to recently act after receiving a significant number of complaints on amount limits. It decided to allow users an increase in the current limit for contactless payments spending per day and raised the maximum amount limit by 33%.

McDonalds, along with many other US vendors, has rolled out contactless payments in all of its restaurants. This technology is now gaining usage worldwide quickly.

5 https://www.irishtimes.com/business/financial-services/contactless-transactions-jump-66-in-first-half-of-2018-1.3684037

6 https://tfl.gov.uk/info-for/media/press-releases/2017/july/one-billion-journeys-made-by-contactless-payment-on-london-s-transport-network

Check Imaging Technology

One of the most notable innovations in retail banking concerns one of its oldest fix-tures—the check! It was way back in 1717 that the Bank of England first began pro-ducing pre-printed checks, and of late there has even been discussion by some financial service providers about retiring this form of payment altogether. However, in the last year many bank customers in the UK have been able to use the new tech-nology of check imaging for the first time, even though this service has already been in use in many countries such as the United States, China, India, France, and many European countries. *Check imaging* works by allowing a customer to take a picture of a check on their mobile device, via their bank's app, and then sending this image directly to the bank. The image is verified, and once approved, the amount of the check is added to the customer's account.

This innovative feature has several more advantages to it than simply saving time depositing a check. One if its main benefits for customers is that it speeds up the check clearing process from approximately six days to just two. It also reduces the risk of a check going astray in the mail, or being ruined by a spilled drink, or even disappearing under a mountain of paperwork.

Conventional checks have been a focus of fraudsters for quite some time. Check fraud represented 35% of all payment fraud in 2018—up for the first time in over a decade as a result of the conversion to chip cards, which makes it harder to success-fully commit fraud on cards with chips.[7]

Could Social Media Shape the Industry?

A recent innovative development by Barclays was to become the first bank to allow customers using the bank's Pingit mobile app[8] to send payments to other people and businesses by simply using their Twitter handles. This has proven to be a par-ticularly convenient method for those needing to send money. It's also useful for recipients because it doesn't require a bank account number, sort code, or routing number to receive the deposit.

Even before social media became a method by which people could transfer money, retail banks were utilizing Facebook and other social networking platforms to communicate with their customers. For example, RBS and NatWest use their Facebook company pages to promote their various product and service offerings, with both banks believing that social media can be a way to assist those customers

---

7 https://www.federalreserve.gov/publications/2018-payment-systems-fraud.htm
8 https://www.pingit.com/

who would not typically use traditional methods to lodge a complaint, or make an enquiry.

Both banks have asserted that were it not for their engagement on social media, they would have been completely unaware that they had dissatisfied customers. However, as of 2018 correspondence between banks and their customers using social media remained modest compared with customers' phone and email usage, or branch visits. It has been reported by large retail banks that on average they respond to about 1,000 Facebook and Twitter messages a week, with these numbers continuing to grow year by year. In early 2016 Lloyds Banking Group[9] came up with a completely new way to use its Facebook company page. The bank overhauled the terms and conditions of its internet banking services and posted a series of videos and infographics on its Facebook company page. By 2019, the bank's Facebook page had nearly 5,400 followers.[10]

Lloyds realized that important documents it was issuing customers weren't being read closely, if at all. This is when Lloyds' innovation lab set about testing formats and techniques that would make it easier for the information to be digested and remembered, in the belief that conditions were ripe for improvement of these documents in the digital era. After initiating the campaign, the bank discovered that customers were much more likely to engage with the new digital version it had created. This resulted in the bank improving its customers' understanding of the many different products and services offered, and it has also contributed to an increase in the number of new accounts.

It has been widely reported over the years that financial institutions aren't the most liked and admired companies out there, with banks often being accused of lacking the human touch. With the digitization of banking, this has increasingly forced banks to make themselves more valuable to their consumers. With retail banks moving towards new digital channels, the already strained relationship between them and their customers may only worsen. Moreover, when financial institutions try to cut costs, branches get shuttered and staff are replaced by chatbots, artificial intelligence, and mathematical algorithms, worsening an already tough job of endearing themselves to their customers.

Instagram provides an innovate way to help banks rehumanize.[11] Facebook is good for sharing information, and Twitter is great for customer service, but Instagram's visual nature gives it a role quite distinct from the others: brand building!

How? One way is for banks to share hidden stories. Brands on social media are often tempted to share every single insignificant detail about themselves, such as

---

9 https://www.lloydsbankinggroup.com/
10 https://www.facebook.com/LBGNews/
11 https://www.instagram.com/lbgtalent/?hl=en

their new app upgrade, new advertisement, and so on. This is not the right way to communicate with customers. It's much better to emotionally engage customers through storytelling.

For instance, people can forget that banks fulfill a critical function in society: lending money to businesses, particularly small businesses that most people use daily, such as mom and pop stores. Banks can take advantage of this by sharing the stories of the small businesses they work with. For example, they can highlight how a loan from the bank enabled a customer company to pursue new avenues that have been successful. Currently, many big-name financial institutions are harnessing the power of Instagram to share such stories, including Citibank, American Express, and U.S. Bank.

The World of Wearable Banking

Financial companies such as Nationwide and Barclaycard have launched wristbands through which customers can make payments. Barclaycard's bPay,[12] now combined with Pingit, is able to load money from a customer's bank card onto their wristbands online. The customer can then use the wristband to buy goods or services at any of the 300,000 select shops around the UK that accept contactless payments. Barclays also allows customers of other banks to use these products, with the bracelets having the advantage of being much harder to misplace than a plastic bank card. Wearing one is so much less cumbersome than carrying a handbag, bulky wallet, or pocketful of change. To date, though, they have had difficulty getting traction, as seen in Figure 7.2. Apple is still driving this market, which was valued at 48.15 billion in 2018 and is expected to almost triple by the end of 2024 with much of its growth in the health services and fitness marketplaces (mordorintelligence.com/industry-reports/global-smart-watches-market-industry).

A Salesforce poll in January 2017 poll showed strong generational differences with 35% of millennials saying they are interested in virtual/branchless banking but only 7% of baby boomers.[13]

Notable Financial Innovators

The following sections discuss some of these financial innovators in detail.

---

12 https://www.bpay.co.uk/
13 Salesforce January 2017, The Financial Board.

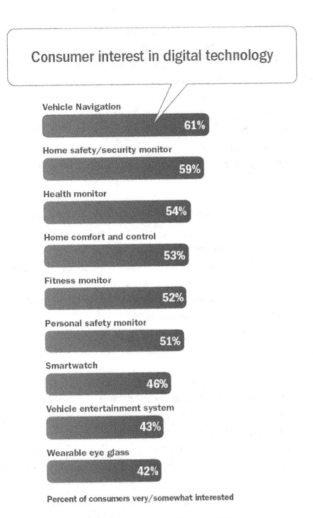

Consumer interest in digital technology

Vehicle Navigation
61%

Home safety/security monitor
59%

Health monitor
54%

Home comfort and control
53%

Fitness monitor
52%

Personal safety monitor
51%

Smartwatch
46%

Vehicle entertainment system
43%

Wearable eye glass
42%

Percent of consumers very/somewhat interested

Figure 7.2: Consumer interest in digital technology.
Source: Accenture © August 2014. The Financial Brand.

Paym

Paym[14] is a mobile payment system in the United Kingdom that has become a helpful financial innovation tool for many people who have signed up for or have been included in their bank's offering of the service since its launch in 2015. The core focus of their system is to allow their users to make various payments to contacts via

---

14 http://paym.co.uk

their mobile phone address book. The company initially saw more than 1 million bank customers registered within 100 days of it the service going live, and nine months later it that had doubled this amount with to more than 2 million registered users. With 15 of the largest banks providing the service on smartphones, users must register to make or receive payments. Thereafter they can do so without going through the process of accessing and sending money has you would a bill.

Almost a third of these payments are set up by people to pay for nominal payments, such as paying back someone who may have bought lunch, reimbursing someone for gas money, contributing to a group gift, or paying a friend back for a movie or concert ticket.

One of the key advantages of the Paym service, is that you are not obliged to use it and it doesn't require giving out your bank account details to someone or to take down those of another person. To date the service has worked for small business customers owing to the ease in using the service. It has the option for users to receive text notifications informing them of completed payments and providing a notification when a payment is scheduled for transfer. This is useful because it helps people avoid having to go through the process of logging into their respective bank accounts, just to see whether a payment has been made or not.

Midata

Midata[15] empowers personal finance comparison choices by giving consumers easier access to their data and helping them use it to choose the right deal. Once signed up users can download all their transaction data from their respective banks from the previous 12 months into one single file. Users can then quickly compare bank accounts to see whether they are getting the best possible value from their current financial service provider.

This pioneering initiative was launched by the UK government alongside many of the major high street banks and British consumer rights groups. Their aim in creating the service was to make banking as transparent as possible, ensuring that bank account holders are getting the best possible deals based on their transactions, charges, and interest payments. If a customer decides to switch an account for a better offer, they can select Midata's Current Account Switch Guarantee service option, which ensures that the process is done in a timely manner and with the confidence that automatic payments will be redirected while the changeover occurs.

Midata not only bolsters competition in the market, it helps customers save money. Midata enables people to have better access to and control over their electronic data.

---

15 https://midata.io/

Are Bank Branches Disappearing?

It's not just hearsay anymore. The reported numbers could not be any clearer: millions of financial consumers are using bank branches much less frequently than ever before. Transactions in the main street outlets of major banks have decreased every year for the past decade, and a 2017 report estimated another 20% reduction in branches by 2022.[16] For many, a range of financial innovations—including ATM/cash machines, cash back from grocery stores, and other digital payment methods—have ended the need to visit the local bank branch regularly.

Although most retail banks have been reducing the number of bank branches (see Figure 7.3), the so-called "death" of the bank branch has been overstated.

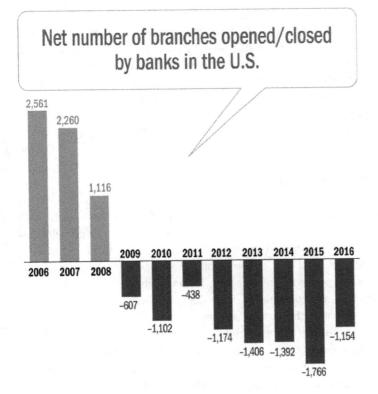

Figure 7.3: Net number of branches opened/closed by banks in the US.
Source: SNL: Business Intelligence Services © September 2016. The Financial Brand.

---

16 https://www.reuters.com/article/us-bank-branches-idUSKBN17Q28N

Proving that branches are not disappearing anytime soon, more than a quarter of the UK's retail bank branches have been refurbished in the past three years, revealing a continued commitment to bricks and mortar. Royal Bank of Scotland (RBS) has refurbished 400 of its branches,[17] and NatWest spent £450 million (approximately $560 million USD) overhauling 1,700 branches.[18]

At the peak of this activity, RBS and NatWest were refurbishing 16 of their bank branches a week. These renovations were not just a new coat of paint, but involved installing new technology into branches to free up staff time, resulting in branch employees being able to spend more time with customers and less time processing administrative work. The two banks have projected that their new "self-service" machines will allow their customers to pay in checks and coins, freeing up an approximate 25% of their bank staff's time.

Bank branches will continue to be around for many more years, and even as more and more people switch to fintech companies that lack a main street presence, there will still be those who will want the security of knowing a bank branch and customer service representative are available for them to visit and speak with. These financial customers tend to place a high value in having face-to-face access to experienced bankers, who understand them and their local market and who can provide recommendations regarding their banking requirements. Even so, these customers are diminishing in numbers, with many of them expected in the future to utilize the option for video conference calls with their respective bankers.

Unlocking Data for Customers

It was only a few years ago that most citizens of the world had to be content with using their mobile phone and tablets on 3G networks. Now 4G is more prevalent as well as reliable high-speed broadband, making it possible for retail banks to offer their customers fast, reliable, and easy-to-use mobile banking. As 5G is implemented, the advantages of greater speed and throughput will make transactions move faster, fewer updates requiring user involvement, and better communications to internet of things devices such as smartwatches and wearables.

Undoubtedly one of the major contributors to the financial revolution that has taken place is the rapid innovation in technology. Financial information is now processed at high speeds, enabling larger volumes of data to be analyzed. Massive data processing that would have taken months to process a decade ago, at a cost of hundreds of thousands of US dollars, today can be processed within hours, at a

---

17 https://www.graven.co.uk/portfolios/royal-bank-of-scotland-retail-banking-concept/
18 https://www.independent.co.uk/voices/maybe-its-time-for-the-natwest-porcelain-pigs-to-go-to-the-slaughterhouse-a6706497.html

fraction of the cost. This availability of cheaper processing at high speeds has been the catalyst for development of many new financial services. Financial institutions can now set up *big data analytics*, enabling rapid analysis of large amounts of information to uncover hidden patterns, unknown correlations, market trends, customer preferences, and other useful business information. Ultimately this could lead to banks providing better financial services to their clients through anticipating their needs and wants and by identifying and mitigating problems before they arise.

Two interlinked types of financial services can further advance data processing and help deliver improved personal financial management. One is often referred to by its abbreviation: PFM.[19] *Personal financial management* software could enable banks to develop features that give customers greater knowledge and insights into how they are spending their money. It may also enable them to break down spending into categories such as food costs, household expenses, and leisure activity outlays. Harnessing this payment data will become more important than ever before for financial customers—most financially savvy people want to know what their present financial position is at any given moment. Humans are generally wired to be competitive in nature, and many of the new PFM systems offer the ability for customers to compare their spending habits to others within their locality, which has proven to be a very popular feature.

An additional service for banks that has many excited is to send highly tailored alerts, notifications, and advice directly to their customers. The enormous potential of this service has still yet to be fully realized, but many financial institutions have begun to comprehend its capability. At present the financial industry uses a standard alert text system; for more specific alerts to be created, banks will need to facilitate this through using data analytics.

An example of the capability your bank could soon have: you have been paying significantly more for energy than similar households on the same street, and those families who have opted for a different energy provider are typically spending 15 to 20% less than you. Through data analysis your bank can identify this and alert you to it, saving you money. Several digital banking experts have expressed enthusiasm for this idea, believing that combining data processing with GPS-enabled mobile phones could be a potential way forward in providing specific timely alerts to customers.

The potential of this technology could be massive in scale. Imagine that you walk into your favorite department store. As you enter you receive an alert from your bank informing you that you are eligible to receive a 10% discount based on your previous spending at the store. Using data in this way could help make customers feel far more secure about their finances and could go a long way toward starting to repair trust in banks, which was damaged after the global financial crisis of

---

19 https://thefinancialbrand.com/73051/banking-guide-personal-financial-management-providers/

2007–2009. At present, only a handful of banks around the world have identified this technology as an opportunity. Some of these banks have even gone as far as developing their own systems to provide the necessary information framework, and are currently piloting their developed mobile apps. The following are just two financial institutions that have understood the importance of unlocking the power of data and already acted on it:

- **Garanti**[20] – A Turkey-based bank offering a mobile app that provides tailor-made recommendations to its customers. It has often been Turkey's most downloaded app on iTunes. This mobile bank app offers customers access to a comprehensive range of personal finance tools and has been built around a set of modules that aggregate wallet, savings, loans, and other specific type offers. The innovative app features a deep social integration across Facebook, Twitter, and FourSquare, allowing Garanti customers to send secure payments to friends via Facebook, tweet relevant offers across their social networks, and even redeem location-based shopping offers while on the move.
- **RBS and NatWest** – Both have developed a similar type of mobile banking app to Garanti, but both have warned customers to not trust the commonly found apps online.[21]

Incremental Change to Total Reinvention

The rapid emergence of financial service innovators has taken many in the world of retail banking by surprise, due to a failure by banks to spot the rapid rise of competitors. Retail banks are facing increased customer volatility—they previously dealt with a generation of customers who would remain loyal and with the same bank for most of their adult lives. As mentioned earlier in this book, the Millennial generation is more likely to switch banks more often than any generation before them. This could ultimately contribute to a "winner takes all" effect, with retail banks that adapt the fastest to new digital technology likely to take significant market share from their competitors.

This increased level of competition banks now face is primarily from agile new fintech startups that are intent on disrupting the entire industry for the better. Two of these emergent new fintech companies are Nutmeg.com[22] and TransferWise,[23] whose businesses have both grown significantly since launching. Both companies have stated that they intend to diversify their service offering by reviewing specific areas of

20 https://www.garanti.com.tr/en
21 https://www.thisismoney.co.uk/money/saving/article-4946222/Don-t-details-new-money-apps-says-NatWest.html
22 https://internationalfintech.com/Company/nutmeg/
23 https://transferwise.com/us

the banking value chain to identify which retail bank offerings can fit within their agile and customer-centric way of doing business. Both have delivered the type of customer financial experience that meets the expectations and needs of today's digitally savvy consumer, in contrast to banks that make incremental improvements to yesterday's processes and were designed for a banking world based on branch visits, telephone, and interactions via mail.

With the rapid rise of fintech companies, traditional retail banks should expect shorter tenure and a much higher turnover on products such as credit cards, loans, and payments. Financial disruptors have also started targeting other services, including checking accounts and mortgages. These two services account for more than half of the revenue of all retail banks today. Since fintech companies have gained a portion of this market, if the trend continues, it could be catastrophic for traditional banks. Accordingly, to survive as they have done for centuries, banks must completely overhaul and reinvent their customer experience process, and offer their customers an exceptional, simple user experience. Additionally, retail

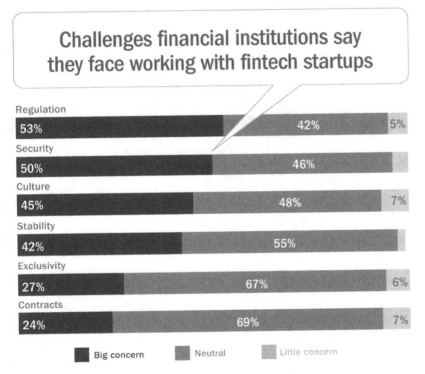

Figure 7.4: Challenges financial institutions say they face working with fintech startups.
Source: Efma-Infosys Finacle © November 2015. The Financial Brand.

banks need to provide customers with a multitude of financial service options, be flexible to their needs, and become transparent with charges and fees.

Of late, quite a few large traditional retail banks have been looking to innovate by partnering with a fintech startup. They are doing this not just for innovation reasons but also as a potential quick fix to potentially help them increase their digital pace of adoption. The handful of companies over the past year that have attempted this collaboration have discovered two major obstacles when trying to combine forces:

1. IT systems between the two parties can prove difficult to integrate. Many of the larger banks still use outdated legacy technology, which often is not compatible with the fintech companies' newer technology.
2. Partnering with a large bank can prove challenging for fintech companies, because when joining forces they then become subjected to the larger bank's regulatory authority (see Figure 7.4) and often struggle to comply fully in this environment.

Chapter 8
International Financial Innovations

New technology cannot simply be put in place. Many inhibiting factors must be addressed as part of an adoption policy. These include regulatory limitations, which are monitored not only nationally but by states, and regulation is not identical for every state. This means that any technology may be subjected to due diligence for regulatory compliance as well as for financial advantage.

In the US, regional differences dictate how banks will be able to advance their digital footprint. For example, banks in the Midwest tend to be more heavily regulated, so that adopting technology could also be more difficult or take more time.[1] Furthermore, the new California Consumer Privacy Act may have an impact on fintechs and banks to the extent that they can use and sell customer information.

Beyond levels of regulation, regional banks also are impacted by price differences, legal issues, and even labor relations.[2]

Moreover, a significant portion of the population is classified as *unbanked*, meaning lack of availability of regional banks. A survey of 35,000 households conducted jointly by the Federal Deposit Insurance Corporation (FDIC)[3] and the US Census Bureau[4] revealed that in 2017, 6.5% of US households were unbanked, representing approximately 8.4 million people. Another 18.7% (24.2 million) were classified as *under-banked*, meaning that beyond rudimentary services such as checking or savings accounts, those families had to seek other products and services outside of the banking system.[5]

Several trends were underway as of 2019 to address these issues. Five global fintech trends are noteworthy:

- **Regulatory sandboxes** — The first trend is development of regulatory sandboxes to deal with outdated rules and regulations. Leading this are regulators themselves; the first sandbox of this type was started in the UK in 2016.
- **Regtech developments** — A second promising trend is expansion of *regtech*, meaning development of regulation through technology. Globally, banks invested $1.4 billion in regtech in the first half of 2018.
- **Cryptocurrency** — Although the crypto world is subject to fraud risk and volatility, its popularity is undeniable. Several countries have placed restrictions and even bans on Bitcoin and others, but cryptocurrencies continue to grow.

---

1 https://link.springer.com/article/10.1007/BF01581896
2 Luger M. & Evans W. (1988). "Geographic differences in production technology." *Regional Science and Urban Economics*, 18: pp. 339–424.
3 https://www.fdic.gov/
4 https://www.census.gov/
5 https://www.fdic.gov/householdsurvey/

https://doi.org/10.1515/9781547401598-008

- **Big tech has moved into finance** — Fintech is moving into banking and other financial spaces aggressively. As online commerce continues to expand through organizations like Amazon.com and Square, regulatory hurdles probably will not be able to slow down the trend.
- **Cashless trends** — An accelerating trend is movement away from cash in transactions. A survey revealed than more than 60% of Americans believe they will see the demise of cash within their lifetimes.[6]

These trends are not restricted to technology. Individuals are also embracing new ways of banking and managing financial transactions. Even so, new regulations have been put in place in response to these trends. In 2017, the EU's banking system faced a "regulatory revolution" largely in response to rapidly expanding fintech influence. These new regulations are designed to expand competition, expand reporting requirements, and fix many flaws in trading. They also have increased capital requirements for banks. These regulations include an updated Payment Services Directive, PSD2,[7] which affects transactions between banks and loosens up banks' ability to control customer account data.[8]

Hundreds of millions of people around the world are harnessing the power of their mobile phones, tablets, and smartwatches to manage their personal finances. Many international financial institutions have already moved ahead with adopting and implementing new technology to improve their services. One type of technology, a favorite of many banks, is the implementation of facial recognition technology[9] to provide a simple way for their customers to access their mobile banking app.

Further types of technology also utilized by financial entities include sophisticated analytical tools that allow customers to set customized financial goals and receive select money-saving offers. One technology which has yet to become prevalent is *augmented reality* (AR)[10] used as a mainstream tool. Examples of its use for banks include enabling customers to find out more about a house they may want to purchase and helping customers navigate their way to the nearest ATM/cash machine simply by holding up the camera on their mobile phones.

The next sections outline a few of these new innovative technologies. International financial service providers listed offer a glimpse into the way millions of people already bank, and indicate which of these potential technologies can be advanced, further disrupting the industry for the better.

6 https://bankingjournal.aba.com/2019/01/five-global-fintech-trends-in-2019/
7 https://ec.europa.eu/info/law/payment-services-psd-2-directive-eu-2015-2366_en
8 https://www.economist.com/finance-and-economics/2017/11/30/europes-banks-face-a-glut-of-new-rules
9 https://us.norton.com/internetsecurity-iot-how-facial-recognition-software-works.html
10 http://www.arsoft-company.com/en/realidad-aumentada/industria/

Australia

The Commonwealth Bank Australia (CBA)[11] unveiled Albert in 2015, the latest industry disruptor to come out of CBA's innovation labs. Two years later, Albert had expanded to over 75,000 terminals and offered 41 apps to businesses and individuals. This initiative was in conjunction with the German tech company Wincor Nixdorf, and US design firm IDEO. Albert is a tablet that completely transforms the way people shop and dine in Australia, as well as simplifies payments for many Australian businesses. The seven-inch Android device is Wi-Fi enabled, accepts contactless and card chip plus PIN payments, and provides options for receipts to be printed or emailed.

Businesses using Albert to date have reported significant reductions in the time it takes people to pay for items. This is due to the ability of those companies that use Albert to serve their customers rapidly with the device. Restaurant goers who use Albert can now easily split their bill up to ten different ways through the device and can choose to pay with cash or a range of different bank or credit card options.

The tablet is also much more than just a payments device. Businesses can download a range of apps for Albert that help make it easier for companies to analyze sales data, pinpoint the busiest periods, and review their customers' spending habits.

Albert allows businesses to have at their fingertips an enormous wealth of data, and the ability to develop strategic insights to improve their experience for customers. Since its release, more than 1,000 software developers have registered to build apps for the platform. More tech-savvy business owners have realized that they can edit Albert's settings in a variety of ways, further allowing tailoring of the tablet to their respective company. An example of this is a restaurant located in Sydney that added an optional tip screen.

Turkey

With almost half of Turkey's population yet to reach their 30th birthday, the country was always going to be one where financial service innovators would gain traction quicker than other, more established markets. It's estimated that more than 90% of people residing in Turkey own a mobile phone, and an astonishing 94% of the country's population has signed up on Facebook. One of Turkey's largest banks, the previously referenced Garanti, has created a mobile banking app considered by many app developers as one of the world's most innovative apps for financial services.

---

11 https://www.commbank.com.au/

Garanti initially led the way in allowing customers to make payments to Facebook friends and contacts in their phone address books via the app. It also was one of the first mobile bank apps allowing users to add all their debit and credit card information, turning phones into mobile wallets in stores throughout the country, as well as providing the ability to purchase goods online and on the go.

One of the app's most innovative features is an option for customers to create a monthly budget based on previous spending habits, and to choose whether to receive notifications based on current spending. For example, if you have spent less than your normal amount by a certain point during the month, Garanti's avatar may suggest that you transfer the surplus to your savings account. Inversely if you have spent more than you should have, the avatar may then offer the ability to receive a loan from the bank. The pioneering bank app also offers promotions tailor-made for their customers, facilitated through their system which identifies users' favorite stores and brands by analyzing their spending habits.

This has enabled the bank to procure exclusive offers for its customers. Users of the bank app can also allow it to harness their mobile devices' GPS technology and to receive specific offer alerts from nearby retailers, restaurants, and businesses. Though some may consider such options as unwanted intrusions into personal life, most people in Turkey do not, and almost all select the option to receive alerts.

These sophisticated features have helped contribute to making the Garanti app an overwhelming success for the bank. Interestingly, many people consider just simply using the mobile bank app to be revolutionary, due to many of its functions being available by talking to the app's avatar, which recognizes voice prompts via cutting-edge voice-activation software.

Iceland

This small Nordic nation may not be the first country that comes to mind when thinking of dynamic financial innovations, but the island's finance industry is transforming rapidly after recovering from the financial crisis several years ago. Virtually the entire population of Iceland utilizes internet banking—considered the highest adoption rate of this service in the world. One explanation is a little-known company based in Reykjavik named Meniga,[12] which specializes in personal finance management software that enables customers to receive considerably more insight into their financial history than ever before.

Headquartered now in London, Meniga was launched in 2009, with the company's primary aim to transform the 21st-century banking system. It's focus is on the Nordic banking and financial services marketplace. Since launching it has

---

12 https://www.meniga.com/

developed software allowing users to obtain highly detailed breakdowns of their spending by assessing through a variety of different categories. Users of the system can set targets for how much they want to spend on these various groupings, and can compare their spending and savings habits with people who live nearby, or equivalent household sizes in Iceland.

Surveys of users of Meniga led to development of an Engagement Index to measure trends in new customers opening accounts and attitudes of existing customers.[13] More than 40% of customers respond that the company has improved their personal financial behavior, with an astounding 90% confirming that they would recommend the company to their friends and family. The company's customer rewards and other technologies offered through its state-of-the-art APIs have now been harnessed by over 75 banks in 2019.[14]

Meniga constantly develops new services based on emerging technology, and best in show at a 2015 Finovate conference in London, the company showcased its innovative new Market Match system,[15] which uses a rolling display. This innovative software system allows retail banks to pass on specific money saving offers from restaurants, retailers, and other service providers, determined by reviewing customers' past spending habits and current location. Meniga's CEO described the future of banking as a world where "banks use data to become a smart and trusted adviser to people in a broader and more meaningful way than what presently occurs today."

New Zealand

The phrase *augmented reality* (AR) may conjure up *Star Wars* type imagery, but this incredible technology has already been harnessed by several banks that want the ability to provide their customers with faster access to financial information faster in ways that are easier to comprehend. In New Zealand one of the country's largest retail banks, Australia-based Westpac,[16] unveiled a dynamic mobile bank app that allows its customers to view their financial information by simply pointing their mobile phone's camera at their bank card. If they have already registered the bank card to the Westpac mobile banking app, the technology provides customers with account balance updates and transaction history. Other financial details are displayed in clear and colorful 3D graphics. The bank app also has quite a few more snazzy options, including how many loyalty points a customer has accrued with

13 https://blog.meniga.com/measuring-meaningful-engagement-3f8999a98d73
14 https://www.meniga.com/about/
15 https://finovate.com/category/meniga/page/5/
16 https://www.westpac.com.au/

various businesses, and warning notifications of number of days left until payment is due for a bill.

Westpac's initial goal in creating the app was to provide its customers with more control and strategic insight into their finances. The bank also realized that many people find personal financial management complex and set the goal of offering customers financial information that was visually pleasing and presented in a fun way. This led to one of Westpac's most innovative features: an AR tool to help customers find the nearest ATM/cash machine. The user holds up their mobile phone's camera, and the app plots a navigation route for the user. Impressively, this feature even works internationally, when a user is attempting to source an ATM/cash machine in a foreign land.

Norway and Sweden

Few countries in the world are as close to cashless societies as these two Nordic nations. It's been calculated that Swedes conduct more transactions per head with credit and debit cards than any other European country, with 31% of Swedish citizens using credit cards for private transactions.[17] This places Sweden at the top of the list when it comes to card payment usage in the world. By the end of 2018, half of Sweden's 1,400 bank branches had stopped accepting cash deposits or withdrawals.[18]

At present, the most downloaded mobile bank app in Sweden is Swish, a mobile payments service set up jointly by six local Swedish banks in 2012. It's estimated that 52% of Swedes use the app, or 5 million users.[19]

The term *swishing* has entered the country's vocabulary. Swish has increased its service offerings, adding the ability for its users to perform a variety of e-commerce transactions.

In Norway, a similar situation has emerged. With encouragement from the government, Norwegian banks strictly comply with policies aimed at reducing the amount of cash circulated within the country. Several years ago, the financial system stopped the acceptance of checks within the country as a form of payment. Nowadays, actual cash used in Norway represents such a small proportion of payments that there have already been numerous debates about whether the country should simply do away with its currency. Recently Norway's central bank, Norges Bank, published research estimating that when taking account of the handling of notes and coins within banks, a typical cash transaction can cost the bank almost

---

17 https://www.statista.com/statistics/663622/credit-card-usage-in-sweden/

18 https://www.nytimes.com/2018/11/21/business/sweden-cashless-society.html

19 https://medium.com/@etiennebr/swish-the-secret-swedish-fintech-payment-company-created-by-nordic-banks-and-used-by-50-of-swedes-cfcf06f59d6f

$1, whereas payment with a bank card only costs about $0.05. This only reinforces Norwegians' view of the benefits of card payments versus cash.

In early 2016, Norway's largest financial services group, DNB, created the first peer-to-peer (P2P) mobile payment solution offered in the country. This mobile app has now become the country's number one downloaded app of all time. Nicknamed Vipps,[20] it was launched in partnership with Tata Consultancy Services (TCS).[21] The app is already being used by more than 100 of the country's banks, with its most popular feature being the ability for users to send short chat messages to each other. One of the main reasons the app has been such a success is due to its exclusive use for account holders of DNB, meaning it can be used by any financial customer within Norway.[22]

Asia

The countries of Japan, Hong Kong, and Singapore are home to some of the world's most innovative bank branches. Thus, when Citi, one of the largest US banking groups, decided to open more than 100 Smart Banking branches across Asia, it knew that state-of-the-art technology would need to be implemented in order to compete with other banks, and to offer its customers a fast, easy-to-use service.

Citi also has also opened Smart Branches in the US market and has become a leader in this field. Citi initially focused on five US cities: Miami, San Francisco, Los Angeles, Chicago, and Philadelphia.[23]

Citi's Asia focus has also been applied widely and met with success, expanding every year.[24] Sparing no expense, Citi brought in the architects behind Apple's retail outlets to design a similarly bright and modern bank branch for them. One of the first things you notice when walking into any one of these Citi branches are large, wall-mounted media screens where customers can view the latest financial market news from around the world. These bank branches also feature extended desks, where customers can log into their personal bank accounts and perform transactions using tablets equipped with keyboards. Dividers are placed along the benches, giving Citi customers the appropriate space for privacy to conduct their banking.

Other noticeable enhancements when visiting these branches are their service browsers, large wall-mounted touch screens that enable customers to source further

---

20 https://quickpay.net/payment-methods/vipps

21 https://www.tcs.com/

22 https://www.instapay.today/article/norways-vipps-gets-adopted-100-banks/

23 https://www.banktech.com/channels/citi-pursues-smart-banking-branches/d/d-id/1296128d41d.html?

24 https://eightinc.com/work/citibank/a-new-ecosystem

information on Citi's financial products and services. Each branch also has screened-off consulting rooms where customers can either talk more discreetly with a member of Citi's staff or videoconference with an employee working elsewhere who perhaps has more specialized knowledge to help a customer.

Another innovative feature is sophisticated ATM/cash machines known as 360 Stations, introduced in Japan in 2010.[25] The machines enable customers to apply for loans, cash checks, and perform many other financial transactions. The bank hopes to equip these stations in the future with the capability to instantly print debit and credit cards for customers, as well as provide a customer service option with the opportunity to speak face-to-face with a customer service adviser 24 hours a day, 7 days a week through the 360 Station machine.

Citi has said that two of its initial goals for these newly designed bank branches was for the advanced technology utilized to, first, contribute to a reduction in staff tasks so that staff can spend more time corresponding with customers, and also to reduce the amount of printed material used by branches, lowering costs and helping the environment. After the successful rollout of launches of the bank branches across the Asian region, Citi turned its focus to an ambitious plan for opening many new Smart Banking branches in the US, India, Brazil, and Saudi Arabia.

United Arab Emirates

In October of 2016, Emirates NBD unveiled its Future Banking Lab, the first of its kind in the United Arab Emirates.[26] This key initiative is part of its digital strategy that will enable and accelerate the development of its next-generation online banking services.

The primary aim of the lab is to increase smart service adoption in the UAE. Its innovative digital branch incorporates both physical and digital designs and three seamlessly connected zones.

The Digital Banking Zone

This zone provides convenient self-service banking facilities where customers can use *intelligent teller machines*, which provide video connections to remote service staff should they require assistance with transactions.

The backdrop of this space is a super-sized digital wall displaying digital animations with a strong visual expression of Emirates NBD's coverage, positioning it

---

25 https://www.citigroup.com/citi/news/2010/100413a.htm
26 The Future Banking Lab: https://allen-international.com/emirates-nbd/

to become the bank of choice in the UAE and demonstrating the brand's commitment to delivering innovative and convenient banking across Dubai and the UAE 24/7.

The Future Banking Zone

Within this zone's space Emirates NBD showcases digital innovations developed with technology partners such as the Visa Connected Car, MasterCard Virtual Shopping Experience, and SAP's Augmented Reality Real Estate and Mortgage Digital Solutions.

The hope is that this changing interactive exhibition space will provide a lab environment for customers to perform trials and collaborate in the development of innovative products and services pre-launch to the UAE market.

The banking group plans to continue evolving and changing this showcase as it works with other future technology partners developing progressive, next-generation digital banking services.

The Relationship Banking Zone

The heart of this zone's space is where Emirates NBD offers customer consultations. The area's contemporary design aim was to provide a relaxed environment for customers to browse the bank's products and services and meet one-on-one with financial advisers.

A quick service desk provides an immediate location for the customer to make enquiries or resolve problems, while the interactive lounge presents tailored digital apps and mobile banking demos to inform and entertain the customer while they wait.

This new innovative venture has ultimately proven to be exceptionally successful for Emirates NBD with non-bank visitor feedback to date indicating that after having visited the project they are 79% more likely to open an account with Emirates NBD based on their experience.

Africa

If you ever visit Nairobi, Kenya, you may be surprised to discover that Kenyans have a very serious culture of mobile payments—far more advanced than many Western countries. You can't escape it, and whether you catch a taxi, buy a drink in a local bar, shop, or purchase groceries, it's almost a given that you will be prompted to pay using M-PESA. By 2018, M-PESA was handling 1.7 billion transactions per year, representing nearly half of Kenya's GDP.

The company's mobile payments system launched in 2007 through the telecoms group, Safaricom,[27] with encouragement from the country's central bank. An economic report published by the World Bank in 2018 estimated that more than 96% of Kenyans are now using their mobile phone to facilitate financial transactions.[28]

M-PESA services include the ability for customers to make transfers, pay bills, and buy phone airtime all through the company's mobile phone app.

Kenya is considered one of the more affluent countries on the continent, but it is by no means the only part of Africa where adoption rates for mobile payment systems are high. For example, studies have indicated that more than half the populations of Gabon and Sudan have already adopted mobile banking services, as have a third of the residents of Algeria, Congo, and Somalia, who have all made an enormous effort to keep up with the mobile revolution taking place.

M-PESA has implemented an ambitious international expansion for the company, and by 2016 had generated over 6 billion transactions, or 528 transactions every second.[29] The business says its value proposition is that e-money is a convenient method of payment for many people living in the developing world. This is due to high crime levels and transportation infrastructure being unreliable or nonexistent, making it difficult for people to travel to their nearest bank branch at a moment's notice. Even in 2018, most countries on the African continent are still considered cash economies, with 80% of all transactions made in cash.[30]

To illustrate just how underdeveloped the banking system is within Africa, it's been reported that in 2017:[31]

- In Sudan there were approximately 4.2 ATM/cash machines for every 100,000 people, compared to 227.8 in North America.
- In Kenya this figure is not that much higher with about 10 ATM/cash machines for every 100,000 individuals.
- South Sudan had the worst ratio of all African nations, with 0.4 one ATM/cash machine for every 100,000 of its citizens.

In many developing economies in Africa, mobile banking is seen as being able to bring financial services to millions of people who have been unbanked for generations.

---

27 https://www.safaricom.co.ke/
28 https://www.worldbank.org/en/news/feature/2018/10/03/what-kenya-s-mobile-money-success-could-mean-for-the-arab-world
29 https://www.vodafone.com/content/index/what/m-pesa.html#
30 https://www.theguardian.com/world/2018/feb/22/kenya-leads-way-mobile-money-africa-shifts-towards-cash-free-living
31 https://data.worldbank.org/indicator/FB.ATM.TOTL.P5

Finally, several other similar African providers are worth mentioning besides M-PESA. These include M-KESHO[32] and M-Shwari.[33] Both companies offer interest on deposits and encourage their customers to strive for greater financial security. Both have a profound belief that they are laying the groundwork for a savings culture within their operating countries, and they hope that this will ultimately lead to a positive impact on the economic development and well-being of the entire continent.

Ireland

A pioneering, innovative loan product in Ireland targeting younger borrowers on Facebook has proven popular in a pilot with 16 of the country's credit unions, which have come together to reach tech-savvy borrowers in their 20s and 30s. The offer? An online loan with a lightning-fast decision. The application process for these loans reportedly takes less than 30 seconds to complete, and all applicants are issued an almost instantaneous response. Irish millennials apparently love the concept, with close to half of them now having taken out at least one Fast-Track Facebook Loan within the past year.

The participating Irish credit unions have stated that the success of the program has far exceeded what they envisioned, with 10% of their total new loan volume stemming from these loans to millennials. They have projected that this percentage will continue to rise and reach 20% in the near future.[34]

The idea came about through Facebook and was initially developed by The Solutions Centre, a credit union think tank based in Dublin, Ireland.[35] This independent innovation incubator was originally spawned by a group of 38 volunteer credit unions that wanted to accelerate the pace of change in Ireland's otherwise motionless banking sector. When the group fielded a research study, it was astonished to find that 57% of respondents said they would prefer not to meet a bank or credit union employee when being assessed for a loan, and would prefer facilitating this online or via an app on their mobile device (see Figure 8.1).

Thus, the loan idea was set in motion, and The Solutions Centre consortium partnered with a diverse assortment of social media companies. Digital marketing experts have created a series of display advertisements exclusively targeting young Irish adults. Clicking one of these ads leads to a simple online application. Currently the Facebook loan program is expanding to include more Irish credit unions, and the expectation is that this will further increase the number of Irish enrolling in this innovative pilot program.

---

32 https://ke.equitybankgroup.com/business/products/ways-to-bank/mobile-banking/m-kesho
33 https://cbagroup.com/m-shwari/how-m-shwari-works/
34 https://www.dublinlive.ie/news/business/credit-unions-started-offering-loans-13213064
35 https://www.solutioncentre.ie/

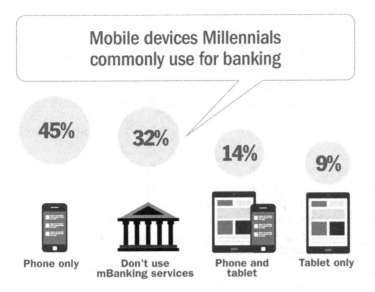

Figure 8.1: Mobile devices Millennials commonly use for banking.
Source: Gemalto © March 2015. The Financial Brand.

Poland

A new financial service company in Poland known as Planet Cash[36] allows customers to withdraw money, check their balances, and transfer funds from ATM/cash machines throughout the country. The system works by using biometric images taken from their customers' fingers, meaning account holders do not even have to insert a bank card to gain access to their accounts. The customer positions themselves directly in front of the ATM/cash machine and then places their finger on a biometrics scanner that uses near-infrared light to capture a vein pattern unique to each person.

The Planet Cash service has been such an overnight success in Poland that the company plans a major expansion to install its technology across a network of 3,700 ATM/cash machines spread throughout the country.[37]

Another market development involves two Polish based banks: Getin Bank[38] and Bank BPH.[39] Both offer biometric security features on their own ATM/cash machines. These two banks have yet to gain any decent market share, primarily due to

---

36 https://en.planetcash.pl/
37 https://en.planetcash.pl/about-us
38 https://www.biometricupdate.com/tag/getin-bank
39 https://www.expat.com/en/guide/europe/poland/14148-opening-a-bank-account-in-poland.html

Planet Cash being the first mover and already winning over the local people with its system. Also, Planet Cash has developed a more user friendly and easy to use system than the two new entrants.

United States

For many people living outside the US, the thought of taking a picture of a check using a mobile device's bank app and submitting that image to their bank, which verifies and processes the payment, may seem a little far-fetched. This technology has existed for more than a decade, allowing American bank customers to deposit checks without visiting their local bank branch.

In October 2014, the United States Congress passed a law making this possible, partly inspired by the terrorist attacks of September 11, 2001, when flights were grounded across the country and the check payment system went offline. When the law passed, financial apps were not quite mainstream, although the legislation had the foresight to include the ability for banks to accept a scanned image of their customer's check. Once smartphones became more prevalent, American bank customers embraced this innovative new technology.

USAA, a Texas-based Fortune 500 diversified financial services group of companies, made history when it became the first bank to allow its customers to access their bank accounts via simply winking into their mobile device's camera.[40] More than 100,000 of USAA's customers use its mobile bank app, with the majority signed up to use the facial and voice recognition features offered. The company has stated that this new technology is considered more secure than passwords and passcodes, which can often fall into the wrong hands or even be guessed by fraudsters.

Facial recognition software obliges the customer to blink at their phone's camera lens. Anyone else who, say, tries to use a photo of the account holder to trick the app, will be denied access. Similarly, for voice recognition, a potential fraudster who acquires a recording of a USAA customer speaking will not be able to gain access either, because the customer will have already secured the mobile bank app with the latest in voice recognition security. Only a short phrase chosen by the customer and spoken will enable access to the bank account. In 2016, USAA reported that almost all their customer biometric logins are successful in the first attempt.

The upside of facial recognition logins is that it typically takes no more than two seconds for a customer to gain access to their account, whereas logging in via voice activation can take up to 20 seconds. The system works by tracking the customer's face and bone structure. It can identify a person even if they had a recent

---

40 https://mobile.usaa.com/inet/wc/usaa_mobile_main?akredirect=true

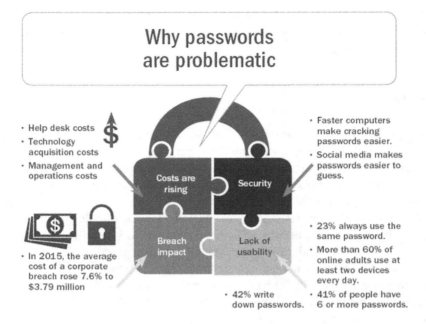

Figure 8.2: Why passwords are problematic.
Source: Deloitte © September 2016. The Financial Brand.

haircut or are wearing sunglasses. The USAA mobile bank app is a godsend for customers who are already overwhelmed by the multitude of login details to remember (see Figure 8.2) for their various accounts. This is what makes USAA's app unique—there are no credentials to memorize, and the system offers more security than other standard mobile banking apps.

Chapter 9
A Digital Blueprint for Banks

As record numbers of financial customers worldwide adapt to digital financial services, most traditional retail banks will need to completely overhaul their antiquated technology infrastructure if they hope to stay relevant and competitive against emerging fintech companies. Some banks will find that they are simply not ready for such an undertaking, and this shouldn't come as a surprise. A report in 2016 stated that retail banks worldwide have on average only digitized approximately one-quarter of their processes, and by 2018 a higher number of regional and smaller banks began acknowledging the need to invest in digital processes in the near future.[1]

Emerging fintech disruptors have seized the initiative within the financial industry after having realized that most banks offered relatively minimal digital financial services and provided only the most basic of customer account services.

Retail banks need to quickly realize that neither financial customers nor fintech companies are going to wait around for them to catch up. If banks delay implementing the latest digital technology, they will find themselves struggling to not only attract potential clients but to retain their current ones. This rapid digital shift can be attributed to customers having become increasingly more financially literate as well as technologically savvy. Most people now have already been introduced to the digital financial revolution through taking advantage of existing innovative technologies in other industries, such as booking flights and vacations, buying books and music, shopping for groceries, and purchasing other goods and services via a variety of digital online channels.

A 2018 study calculated that digital transformation created bank investment of nearly $10 billion. This reveals that banks understand the relationship between digital transformation and customer satisfaction. As a growing number of customers use digital bank services, increasing levels of overall profit are expected to result.[2]

Many banks may be discouraged by the initial upfront cost to digitally adapt, but they need to consider the benefits, including significant cost reductions over the long term. This can be achieved by retail banks leveraging the digital shift and transforming the way in which they process and serve their clients. It's also vitally important during this period of rapid change for the financial industry that traditional retail banks get their digital transformation right the first time. Banks operate within a fiercely competitive environment and cannot afford to waste time and

---

1 https://www.mobilearth.com/mobile-banking-news/digital-transformation-banks-digitization-2018
2 https://www2.deloitte.com/insights/us/en/industry/financial-services/digital-transformation-in-banking-global-customer-survey.html#endnote-2

https://doi.org/10.1515/9781547401598-009

money implementing new IT systems. They are competing for market share not just with other retail banks, but with new online digital banking firms and emerging fin-tech companies.

You may be wondering why some retail banks are still not aggressively updating their digital offerings and consider this digital update a no-brainer. One of the main reasons identified for their slower transformation into digital banking is that senior bank executives have tended to view digital transformation too narrowly. They often see it as a stand-alone front-end feature, such as a mobile bank app or an online product-comparison chart. Commonly lost within management's view of digital transformation are needed changes to frontline customer service tools, internal processes, data analytics, and staff capabilities. These changes should be stitched together for a bank to have one coherent working front-to-back banking system. Senior managers need to realize that although the digital journey may begin through an online form or payment calculator, it does not remain there for long, as anyone who has taken on a mortgage can attest. Instead, the onerous documentation requirements and significant manual intervention that characterize a typical retail bank's mortgage process will soon emerge. This is especially jarring to those financial customers accustomed to more streamlined interactions with non-banking entities. The old guard of banking will often be quick to point out that security and risk concerns are justification for their slow approach in transforming digitally, but this is in complete contrast to other industries. For example, the airline industry, arguably beset by even stronger and more pressing risk concerns, has in the last decade automated almost every aspect of its customer experience without compromising safety. Retail banks can achieve the same benefits, and efforts are more than likely to pay for themselves in the long run.

Digital Banking Value?

In addition, some retail banks are unable to commit to a complete overhaul of their technology systems. New digital initiatives can be implemented in the interim to improve the banks' digital service offering. An example of this could be a bank deploying a simple account registration page on its website, allowing prospective customers to complete online applications from any location in the world, as opposed to having to visit a bank branch or even print, complete, sign, and then mail the application forms to the bank.

Another simple innovative example that could easily be implemented by any retail bank is to provide clients with the ability to be able to schedule a videoconference with one of their bank's specialists. This could enable customers to save time by not having to travel to a local bank branch for a face-to-face meeting. Moving forward, it's recommended that retail banks carefully plan the evolution of digital transformation, and especially place emphasis on the success rate of newly implemented digital products or services. At the same time, banks should also pursue a broader range of strategic opportunities. Some of these could possibly include the following:

- Improved customer targeting via digital marketing (see Figure 9.1) and micro segmentation
- Engaging in dynamic tailored pricing and product bundling
- Establishing third-party integration with websites such as Facebook and LinkedIn
- Product white-labeling

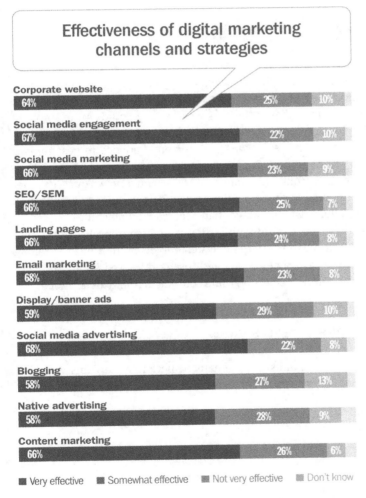

Figure 9.1: Effectiveness of digital marketing channels and strategies.
Source: Salesforce © September 2015. The Financial Brand.

- Appropriate distribution via aggregators
- Development of distinctive mobile and website sales offerings

Although going digital doesn't have to mean spending millions of dollars overhauling bank IT systems. There will likely be areas requiring significant investment, but in other areas systems may already be in place and can immediately form part of the digital strategy. If none of the elements already exist, banks will need to better leverage themselves, make targeted investments which should be prioritized in order of return for the bank, and make use of cases and examples like those proposed in the following sections.

Maximize Use of Existing Technology

Many banks have already implemented and widely deployed imaging and workflow systems, online servicing, capacity-management software, interactive-voice-response systems, and other connectivity and work-management technologies. However, most banks are not utilizing them as well as they could. An example of this is a bank based in Europe that installed a high-resolution imaging platform but never fully enforced its use. The result was that customer service representatives continued to send documentation by fax, and low image quality led to significant inefficiencies regarding Anti-Money Laundering (AML)[3] and Know Your Customer (KYC)[4] policies. This not only increased the time taken for due diligence, it discouraged many prospective clients who no longer had access to fax machines.

When addressing these types of difficulties that may arise from the installation of any new system, what needs to occur is a systematic evaluation of the existing capabilities. This should be completed along with usage rates and identifying barriers to adoption for staff before the best possible solution is finally determined.

Apply Minor Technology Interventions

A significant number of retail banks have generated performance gains with surprisingly small targeted investments. Three examples demonstrate this strategic approach:

---

3 https://www.experian.com/lp/decision-analytics/anti-money-laundering-solutions.html?
msclkid=4854a6344f2b1562cbe3fa8039c7fe9c
4 https://www.experian.com/lp/decision-analytics/know-your-customer-compliance.html?
msclkid=547eed6f50bc1a2dd77db1db279cc7a6

1. Initiate a wider deployment of tools such as e-forms and workflow systems, which can be set up relatively quickly and often without the need to perform deep integration into complex legacy systems.
2. Bring together relationship managers and underwriters with the IT department to facilitate the design of a new streamlined and user-friendly online loan application (see Figure 9.2). This form can then be developed to automatically adapt to data being input, and once submitted this helps guide the underwriters and the risk processes they should follow.
3. Speed up mortgage decisions by tweaking existing application documents. These online forms could be developed with information pertaining to minimum down payment thresholds as well as ratings data. When the bank receives the application, the data can be assessed more rapidly and with less manual intervention due to the system having computed from the applicant's data whether the bank should proceed with the mortgage decision.

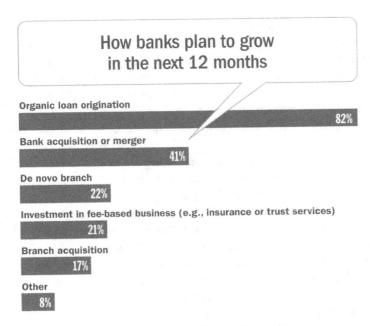

Figure 9.2: How banks plan to grow in the next 12 months.
Source: Bank Director © September 2015. The Financial Brand.

Identify Areas for Sweeping Transformation

There are specific areas in any retail bank requiring the pursuit of comprehensive digital transformation. Alternatively, instead of trying to automate every aspect of the bank's processes or product and service offerings, the bank may select a few key areas with the potential to drive the most capacity consumption, providing the bank with the greatest return over the medium to long term.

Although it's extremely important that retail banks modernize, there is no need to apply all of a bank's resources to building the most sophisticated digital banking empire online just for the sake of it. Some banks find that when they start the process of systematically mapping their entire processes for automation, fewer than ten processes represent the bulk of full-time-employee activity. If a bank decides to embark on this process and finds itself in a similar situation, they are among the fortunate few that can make other investments that are not digitally oriented.

Cross-Selling in the Digital Era

To be effective at cross selling in the digital age, banks need to be able to make personalized offers and initiate interactions based on a clear, up-to-date understanding of their customers. They need a technology infrastructure that can break down channel silos, collect information, and centralize the data to create an offer repository where what is offered, rejected, and accepted is known. It's vital that banks get a 360-degree view of their customers regarding their transaction history and their interactions with the bank, both live and virtual, as well as be able to collect relevant customer data from outside the bank.

This data must be visible and accessible across all channels, so that everyone within the organization is on the same page. Also, banks need to be adaptable and have a technology infrastructure that addresses what is important to the financial consumer, that can capture additional consumer needs, as well as suggest in real time the appropriate solutions based on these data points.

When a bank is undertaking something that isn't in the best interest of its customer, it's not in the bank's best interest either. Effective cross-selling starts with knowing what is important to the bank's customers and following up with relevant offers supported by the ability to refine those offers in real time. To be able to facilitate this, banks of the future will need to access crucial data on consumer financial behaviors, understand when to engage with them, and know when to approach customers when they are most receptive to receiving offers for the bank's products and services.

Chapter 10
Human Resources in the Digital Era

There is no amount of technology that will help a retail bank if that bank does not address the people issues driven by digital transformation. Success in the digital age requires more than just rethinking technology; it requires a complete rethinking of the organizational bank model, particularly when it comes to skills, structure, incentives, and performance management. The suggested points in the following sections can assist the bank's staff with the required digital changes that affect human resources.

Optimizing Structure and Incentives

There is more than one way to reorganize a bank around digital change. Some banks decide on appointing a *head of digital* and give that person profit-and-loss responsibility to smooth the transition. Other banks have instead used a *center-of-excellence* (COE)[1] model to develop offerings that the rest of the business can deploy. Either model can work well, but the bank will need to make a concerted effort to realign the incentives of all staff to ensure complete buy-in regarding the new process. Problems can arise by creating a COE without giving the business digital targets. This can lead to a lot of technology being successfully built or implemented but with limited drive and pull for adoption. In extreme cases the wrong functionality is developed, and although it may be an exciting concept to demonstrate, if ultimately it creates no bottom-line impact or improvement for the bank, it should be considered a complete waste of time and resources.

This is why a cost-benefit analysis should always be part of implementing any new systems, including digital transformation. The analysis should include at a minimum the following questions:

1. Is the proposed change most likely to improve customers' experience in dealing with bank transactions?
2. Can the change be explained easily?
3. What internal training is required and what is the time needed for training?
4. How much will it cost and is it worth the investment?

---

1 https://whatis.techtarget.com/definition/center-of-excellence-CoE

https://doi.org/10.1515/9781547401598-010

Emphasizing Business Outcomes

Banks may decide that the best way to manage the progress of their digital transformation is by tracking activity metrics, such as the number of app downloads or online banking logins. However, often these metrics are completely inadequate when measuring business value. Banks should instead set clear aspirations for value outcomes, looking at productivity, servicing-unit costs, and lead-conversion rates, and linking these explicitly to digital investments. Only after this has been properly defined will the collective focus of the bank's governance and management personnel be on the right track needed to fully capture the potential value available.

Devising a New Strategic Vision for Staff

Essential to these changes is devising an entirely new strategic vision for the bank's staff to assist them with navigating the digital reality they now face. The strategy should include an outline of the expected activities that employees need to spend their time on to gain skills, as well as an explanation of how best to work with these newly implemented technologies.

What may become apparent through new digital transformations within a bank is that the change will diminish the importance of some people's roles. This is why so many people view change as a threat and resist making the required changes. They fear that change will adversely affect them. There may be a shift in focus for the employee toward facilitating higher-value tasks, giving them the potential to create exciting new opportunities for business development and growth. For example, with the change, relationship managers could be able to spend less time capturing customer details, and more time giving valuable financial advice to customers, improving their experience with the bank.

In this digital era, a bank's senior leaders and executives will need to understand of the technical capabilities available to them, and how these can affect operational processes. This is likely to become a prerequisite for effectively managing in this new period of banking. A good suggestion for hiring a senior executive within the bank is to ask prospective candidates to demonstrate during the interview process that they are knowledgeable in how technology can be leveraged to address the myriad of commercial retail banking challenges. Their answer will reveal whether the candidate understands how the industry is radically evolving, and is familiar with the various types of strategic initiatives needed just to stay competitive.

The bank cannot rely on bringing in new talent from digitally savvy industries to transform operations. Even though new talent can provide an important stimulus, serving digital needs becomes a new management competency across the entire organization, not just a job for a select few employees.

Chapter 11
The Future of Banking

There is no doubt that new technological innovations are profoundly changing the way in which financial services are conducted around the world. Not only has the banking industry been redefined, but expectations of financial customers have been dramatically altered with it. At present, traditional retail banks are being forced to evolve not only to secure existing sources of revenues, but also to find potential new ones. Adding even further complexity to the challenges facing banks is that financial customers are now taking ever-increasing control of their personal finances. As people move from researching to eventually selecting a product or service, they are showing an increased propensity to switch from website to website and from channel to channel, questioning service providers, reading online reviews, and seeking advice on various social networks as they go through the process to determine the best deal available to them.

As the larger more established high street and main street banks continue migrating to a digital banking world, this will lead to further fragmentation in the financial services market. Digitalization of financial service is accompanied by a significant shift in power and influence from existing financial services providers to their customers and other parties and intermediaries. As these banks make these changes, they find that migrating to this digital world proves difficult, due to decades-old back office legacy technology systems.

The expenditure required for digitizing customer-facing channels when IT systems require manual interventions (or even extensive add-ons just to be able to connect everything) is expensive. However, the way retail banks will be able to potentially achieve the agility and openness necessary to thrive in this financial service revolution will be through equipping themselves with a completely new set of innovative digital solutions, including the following:

- Updating multichannel customer experience platforms
- Ensuring operational processes have been streamlined with technology
- Implementing advanced analytics for CRM, business development, and marketing
- Providing applications via platforms such as Apple and Google stores

All the threats banks face come at an inopportune time due to the fact that mature markets experience stagnant growth. This is coupled with decreasing profit margins due to the competitive pricing of new entrants, and with financial customer loyalty becoming increasingly more tenuous (see Figure 11.1).

However, the data suggests that here suggests that over the past few years that would have been massive changes in the customer mix, but as a 2018 survey at blog. accessdevelopment.com/the-ultimate-collection-of-loyalty-statistics shows, 61% of the US female bank customers stay with their bank over five years. As we have pointed

https://doi.org/10.1515/9781547401598-011

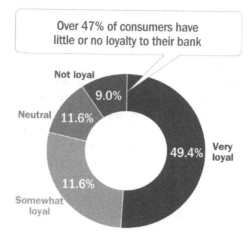

Figure 11.1: Over 47% of consumers have little or no loyalty to their bank.
Source: NGDATA © March 2015. The Financial Brand.

out, what people say and what they actually do are quite different. Even so, this same survey points out that 61% of bank customers considered it very important to have the ability to manage multiple loyalty programs with the same mobile wallet, but only 21% of providers offer this service.

For traditional retail banks to remain relevant in this highly competitive market, they need to nurture the customer experience and move quickly to provide non-traditional services wished for by their customers. By constantly listening to market demands for convenient, simple-to-use, easy-to-understand banking products and services that integrate seamlessly into their customers' lives. Taking this into account, several areas should be considered of the utmost importance for retail banks to not only focus on but to facilitate going forward:

- **Go beyond banking** — Deepen customer relationship by offering solutions that go beyond banking products and address all aspects of the important stages of customers' lives. This basic *customer service* mindset is too often missing in banks and other service industries, but it makes a significant difference.
- **Make it easy** — Grow customer-centric digital platforms and enable the banks sales team to give customers real-time, anytime access to products, services, support, and advice. This often demands refocused training in light of the newly changed industry and the keen competitive forces at work.
- **Make it personalized** — Leverage market and customer insights to build relationship-based products and pricing that is delivered seamlessly across all channels. This demands a combination of a type of hands-on, face-to-face interaction and at the same time increased digital processes.

- **Keep customers' interests at heart** — This is not only best way to build a re-ciprocal, long-lasting loyal relationship, it's the *only* way. More than any digital improvement or convenience, keeping customers at the top of the priority list is essential.
- **Make trust a top priority** — Promote transparency in all bank dealings and transactions and take proactive steps to protect customers from data, privacy, and cybersecurity threats.

Despite the varied challenges retail banks face, they still possess an inherent compet-itive advantage in this digital era. This derives from their larger customer bases, vast amounts of customer and transaction data, and years of built-up valuable know-how in the fields of payments, security, compliance, and financing. These competencies are difficult to replicate by financial start-up firms because they will act as financial intermediaries, and banks will continue to have vast experience when it comes to the transactions carried out between their customers and merchants.

This transactional information is one of the greatest assets of retail banks and will continue to be for many more decades. This information allows banks to better understand their customers, provide them with value-added services, and facilitate financial services in a variety of new ways. Financial service innovators are increas-ingly becoming disruptive to the banking industry, so banks will need to ensure they move much more swiftly than before, and keep abreast of the latest in digital changes.

Those banks that fully embrace these rapid digital changes and make a con-certed effort to carry on adapting, evolving, and innovating will in the end ensure their continued growth and relevance in the banking industry well into the future. Innovative disruptors such as Apple, Amazon, and Google have created new worlds of customer experiences that were not even imagined in the past. Today, technolog-ical advancements are so firmly entrenched in peoples' everyday lives that it's hard to imagine life without them.

Retail banks and fintech companies have similar opportunities to surprise, de-light, revolutionize, and ultimately normalize new ways of conducting financial services. Leveraging opportunities enabled by digital technologies will be a critical part of the path forward for banks; however, their current most pressing need is to shift away from defending the old way of banking to going on the offensive and producing innovative financial technologies of their own, ensuring they are back at the forefront of providing disruptive banking solutions of their very own.

List of Sources

Abel, Andrew & Bernanke, Ben (2005). *Macroeconomics* (5th ed.). New York: Pearson, pp. 522–532.

Accenture
"The Boom in Global Fintech Investment" (PDF). (https://www.cbinsights.com/research-reports/
Boom-in-Global-Fintech-Investment.pdf)
The Everyday Bank – A New Vision for the Digital Age (PDF report) (https://www.accenture.com/us-
en/insight-everyday-bank-new-vision-digital-age-banking)
(https://newsroom.accenture.com/archive.cfm)
"Remaking Customer Markets: Unlocking Growth with Digital." (http://www.accenture.com/
SiteCollectionDocuments/us-en/landing-pages/customermarkets/Accenture-Remaking-Customer-
Markets-Unlocking-Growth-Digital.pdf)
survey. (PDF) (https://www.accenture.com/us-en/~/media/Accenture/Conversion-Assets/
Microsites/Documents17/Accenture-2015-North-America-Consumer-Banking-Survey.pdf)
Results of Accenture survey of 115 senior level banking industry executives across 19 countries.
(PDF) (https://www.accenture.com/t20160203T003336__w__/us-en/_acnmedia/Accenture/
Conversion-Assets/DotCom/Documents/Global/PDF/Digital_2/Accenture-Everyday-Bank-New-
Vision-For-Digital-Age.pdf)

Access Development
https://blog.accessdevelopment.com/2018-customer-loyalty-statistics#bank

Ad Age. "Millennials Want to Party With Your Brand But On Their Own Terms." (http://adage.com/
article/digitalnext/millennials-party-brand-terms/236444)

Affirm.com
https://www.affirm.com/press/releases/affirm-unveils-updated-brand-new-logo-and-shopping-fea
tures-in-time-for-the-holidays/

Alibaba
https://www.alibabagroup.com/en/global/home

Ajilore, Joseph. "Skype's first employee: How Taavet Hinrikus left Skype and founded TransferWise."
YHP. (http://yhponline.com/2012/03/20/taavet-hinrikus-transferwise)

Allenovery
http://www.allenovery.com/publications/en-gb/lrrfs/uk/Pages/The-Banking-Reform-Act-2013.
aspx

All Things Distributed
https://www.allthingsdistributed.com/2018/12/introducing-the-aws-stockholm-region.html

Amazon.com
https://www.amazon.com/s/?ie=UTF8&keywords=fsa+approved&tag=mh0b-20&index=aps&hva
did=78683853869722&hvqmt=p&hvbmt=bp&hvdev=c&ref=pd_sl_10p8xhnlhc_p

American Banker
https://www.americanbanker.com/opinion/regional-banks-are-spending-heavily-on-tech-is-it-enough
https://www.americanbanker.com/opinion/banks-are-running-out-of-time-to-regain-public-trust

https://doi.org/10.1515/9781547401598-012

Arner, Douglas W., Janos Barberis, Ross P. Buckley. "The Evolution of Fintech: A New Post Crisis Paradigm?" (https://papers.ssrn.com/sol3/papers.cfm?abstract_id=2676553)

ArSoft
http://www.arsoft-company.com/en/realidad-aumentada/industria/

Australian Financial Review Magazine. "Sydney Fintech hub based on London's Level39 coming next April." BRW. (http://www.afr.com/it-pro/sydney-fintech-hub-based-on-londons-level39-coming-next-april-20141126-11updp)

AWS. "AWS Global Infrastructure." (https://aws.amazon.com/about-aws/global-infrastructure)

AWS. "What is Cloud Computing?" (https://aws.amazon.com/what-is-cloud-computing)

Bancorp
https://www.thebancorp.com/about/news/2017/07/team-updates-07262017/

Bank for International Settlements. "Monitoring adoption of Basel standards." (http://www.bis.org/bcbs/implementation/bprl1.htm)

Banking Journal
https://bankingjournal.aba.com/2019/01/five-global-fintech-trends-in-2019/

Banking Tech
"Citi rolls out 'branchless' ATMs in Asia" (http://www.bankingtech.com/60402/citi-rolls-out-%E2%80%9Cbranchless%E2%80%9D-atms-in-asia)
"DNB's P2P mobile payments app is Norway's No 1." (http://www.bankingtech.com/459272/dnbs-p2p-mobile-payments-app-is-norways-no-1)

Bank Tech
https://eightinc.com/work/citibank/a-new-ecosystem

Bankrate
https://www.bankrate.com/banking/americas-top-10-biggest-banks/#slide=1

Basel III
https://www.bis.org/bcbs/basel3.htm

Basis Point
https://thebasispoint.com/many-mortgage-loan-officers-companies-u-s-2q2017/

Bátiz-Lazo, B. and P. Wardley. Banking on change: information systems and technologies in UK high street banking, 1919–1969. *Financial History Review*, 14(02). http://dx.doi.org/10.1017/s0968565007000534

Behalf.com
https://www.behalf.com/about/

Benzinga
https://benzingafintechawards.com/vote-2018/iex/

Betterment.com
https://www.betterment.com/press/newsroom/the-fintech-250-the-top-fintech-startups-of-2018/

Biometric Update
https://www.biometricupdate.com/tag/getin-bank

Bitcoin
https://bitcoin.org/en/

Bitcoin Market Journal
https://www.bitcoinmarketjournal.com/how-many-people-use-bitcoin/

Bloomberg
"Skrill Holdings Limited: Private Company Information." http://www.bloomberg.com/research/
stocks/private/snapshot.asp?privcapId=118905485)
"How the ATM Revolutionized the Banking Business." (https://www.bloomberg.com/view/articles/
2013-03-27/how-the-atm-revolutionized-the-banking-business)

bPay
https://www.bpay.co.uk/

British Bankers' Association, Reforms since the Financial Crisis (PDF)
(https://www.bba.org.uk/news/reports/bba-briefing-reforms-since-the-financial-crisis/#.
WAcLduBn2Uk)

Brito, Jerry and Andrea Castillo (2013). "Bitcoin: A Primer for Policymakers" (PDF). Mercatus Center.
George Mason University. (https://www.mercatus.org/publication/bitcoin-primer-policymakers)

Brookings. "Brookings-Financial Crisis" (PDF).
(https://www.brookings.edu/research/the-origins-of-the-financial-crisis)

Bryant, Martin. "Money may make the world go round, but at what cost?" BBC.
(http://www.bbc.com/news/business-31639262)

Casinos Online. "Online Casinos that Accept Skrill / Moneybookers."
(http://www.casinosonline.com/withdrawal-methods/moneybookers)

Cassandra Report
https://cassandra.co/

Cato Institute
https://www.cato.org/publications/policy-analysis/repeal-glass-steagall-act-myth-reality

CBA Group
https://cbagroup.com/m-shwari/how-m-shwari-works/

Census Bureau
https://www.census.gov/

Centre for Policy Studies
"Big Bang 20 years on" London: Centre for Policy Studies. October 2006, at https://www.cps.org.uk/
files/reports/original/111028101637-20061019EconomyBigBang20YearsOn.pdf

Chen, Y. Google Inc.: A Case Study. SSRN Electronic Journal.
(http://dx.doi.org/10.2139/ssrn.1976444)

Cheung Kong Graduate School of Business. "Can Alibaba's Ant Financial Disrupt China's Financial Industry?" (http://knowledge.ckgsb.edu.cn/2015/08/05/finance-and-investment/can-alibabas-ant-financial-disrupt-chinas-financial-industry)

Chu, Lenora. "What PayPal does with your money." CNNMoney. (http://money.cnn.com/2008/02/26/smbusiness/paypal_float.fsb)

Citigroup
https://www.citigroup.com/citi/news/2010/100413a.htm

CNBC
"HSBC customers can open new bank accounts using a selfie." (http://www.cnbc.com/2016/09/05/hsbc-customers-can-open-new-bank-accounts-using-a-selfie.html)
https://www.cnbc.com/2017/07/21/the-crazy-growth-of-bank-fees.html

CNN Money. "What is Bitcoin?"
(http://money.cnn.com/infographic/technology/what-is-bitcoin)

Coin Market Cap
https://coinmarketcap.com/

Commonwealth Bank
https://www.commbank.com.au/

Competition and Markets Authority. UK Government – Banking summary. (PDF) (https://www.gov.uk/government/uploads/system/uploads/attachment_data/file/470032/Banking_summary_of_PFs.pdf)

Competition and Markets
https://competitionandmarkets.blog.gov.uk/2018/02/06/retail-banking-remedies/

Congress.gov
https://www.congress.gov/bill/111th-congress/house-bill/1/text

Consumer Finance
https://www.consumerfinance.gov/policy-compliance/rulemaking/final-rules/code-federal-regulations/

Cornell University
https://www.law.cornell.edu/uscode/text/12/1467a

CreditCards.com
https://www.creditcards.com/credit-card-news/how-we-apply-for-credit-cards.php

Credit Soup
https://www.creditsoup.com/articles/2018/12/credit-card-companies/

Critical Reviews. "Financial Services Authority approves TransferWise without limits." (http://www.critical-reviews.com/transferwise-investment)

Cyber Cemetery
https://cybercemetery.unt.edu/archive/fcic/20110310172443/http://fcic.gov/

Daily Telegraph
Wallace, Tim (December 29, 2015). "Are challenger banks the saviours of British banking?" *The Daily Telegraph*.

Danciulescu, D. Optimization of a Google AdWords Campaign: Case Study. SSRN Electronic Journal. (http://dx.doi.org/10.2139/ssrn.1004059)

Davies, G. (1994) "A History of Money from Ancient Times to the Present Day," Cardiff, UK, University of Wales Press.

DB Research. "New solutions to an old problem." (PDF) (https://www.dbresearch.com/PROD/DBR_INTERNET_EN-PROD/PROD0000000000344173/SME±financing±in±the±euro±area%3A±New±solutions±to±an±old±problem.PDF)

Deloitte
https://www2.deloitte.com/insights/us/en/industry/financial-services/digital-transformation-in-banking-global-customer-survey.html#endnote-2

de Ternay, Guerric. "Fintech Revolution: How Startups Are Changing Finance." BoostCompanies. (https://boostcompanies.com/fintech)

Dollar Times
https://www.dollartimes.com/inflation/inflation.php?amount=7&year=1933

Drum, Kevin. "The Repeal of Glass-Steagall." Mother Jones. (http://www.motherjones.com/kevin-drum/2009/03/repeal-glass-steagall)

DTCC
http://www.dtcc.com/regulatory-compliance/csdr

Dublin Live
https://www.dublinlive.ie/news/business/credit-unions-started-offering-loans-13213064

Dutta, M. Effectiveness of Online Advertising on Social Networking Sites – A Case Study on Facebook. SSRN Electronic Journal. (http://dx.doi.org/10.2139/ssrn.2357623)

EC Europa
https://ec.europa.eu/info/business-economy-euro/banking-and-finance/financial-supervision-and-risk-management/managing-risks-banks-and-financial-institutions/deposit-guarantee-schemes_en
https://ec.europa.eu/info/law/law-topic/eu-banking-and-financial-services-law_en
https://ec.europa.eu/info/law/payment-services-psd-2-directive-eu-2015-2366_en

The Economist
Investment banking – Is there a future? (http://www.economist.com/node/12274054)
https://www.economist.com/finance-and-economics/2017/11/30/europes-banks-face-a-glut-of-new-rules

Edelman
"Edelman – Trust In Financial Services" (http://www.edelman.com/insights/intellectual-property/trust-2013/trust-across-sectors/trust-in-financial-services)

Edelman. "2015 Edelman Trust Barometer Finds Trust in Financial Services." (http://www.edelman. com/news/2015-edelman-trust-barometer-finds-trust-in-financial-services-outpaces-the-tech-indus try-to-innovate-electronic-and-mobile-banking) https://www.edelman.com/sites/g/files/aatuss191/files/2019-03/2019_Edelman_Trust_ Barometer_Global_Report.pdf?utm_source=website&utm_medium=global_report&utm_cam paign=downloads, p. 47

Eight Inc https://eightinc.com/work/citibank/a-new-ecosystem

Elliott, Larry, economics editor of *The Guardian*. "Three myths that sustain the economic crisis" (Blog). *The Guardian*. (https://www.theguardian.com/business/economics-blog/2012/aug/05/eco nomic-crisis-myths-sustain)

eMoney Advice http://emoneyadvice.com/mif-ifr/

Encyclopedia.com https://www.encyclopedia.com/history/encyclopedias-almanacs-transcripts-and-maps/national- bank-act-1863

Entrepreneurial Thought Leader Speaker Series: ECorner – "Paypal is Not a Bank." (http://ecorner. stanford.edu/authorMaterialInfo.html?mid=1036.)

"European Banking Overseas, 19th-20th Century." *Austrian Economic History Review*, 46(1), 99-101. (http://dx.doi.org/10.1111/j.1467-8446.2006.00156.x)

EY. "The Way We Bank Now: World of Change." (PDF) (http://www.ey.com/Publication/ vwLUAssets/EY-The-way-we-bank-now-A-world-of-change/$FILE/EY-and-BBA-The-way-we-bank- now-A-world-of-change.pdf)

Expat https://www.expat.com/en/guide/europe/poland/14148-opening-a-bank-account-in-poland.html Facebook statistics (http://newsroom.fb.com/company-info)

Experian https://www.experian.com/lp/decision-analytics/anti-money-laundering-solutions.html?msclkid= 4854a6344f2b1562cbe3fa8039c7fe9c https://www.experian.com/lp/decision-analytics/know-your-customer-compliance.html?msclkid= 547eed6f50bc1a2dd77db1db279cc7a6

FCA https://www.fca.org.uk/ https://www.fca.org.uk/firms/remuneration https://www.fca.org.uk/firms/crd-iv/remaining-crd-iii https://www.fca.org.uk/news/speeches/fair-and-effective-markets-review https://www.handbook.fca.org.uk/handbook/BCOBS.pdf

FdataGlobal https://fdata.global/

FDIC
https://www.fdic.gov/
https://www.fdic.gov/householdsurvey/

Federal Reserve
https://www.federalreservehistory.org/essays/riegle_neal_act_of_1994

Lakshmi Balasubramanyan and Joseph G. Haubrich (2013). "What Do We Know about Regional Banks? An Exploratory Analysis," Federal Reserve Bank of Cleveland, working paper no. 13–16
https://www.frbatlanta.org/education/classroom-economist/fractional-reserve-banking/econo mists-perspective-transcript

Federal Reserve Bank of Minneapolis, Facts and Myths about the Financial Crisis of 2008
(https://www.minneapolisfed.org/research/working-papers/facts-and-myths-about-the-financial-cri sis-of-2008)
https://www.federalreserve.gov/publications/2018-payment-systems-fraud.htm

The Financial Brand
"Are Banks Still Relevant?" (https://thefinancialbrand.com/61120/banking-fintech-trust-relevancy)
"Why Banks Need Instagram" (https://thefinancialbrand.com/61586/bank-marketers-need-instagram)
https://thefinancialbrand.com/65210/banking-customer-technology-growth-investment-trends/
https://thefinancialbrand.com/73051/banking-guide-personal-financial-management-providers/

Financial Crisis Inquiry Commission. *Final Report of the National Commission on the Causes of the Financial and Economic Crisis in the United States* (PDF). (https://www.gpo.gov/fdsys/pkg/GPO-FCIC/content-detail.html)

Financial Engineer
https://thefinancialengineer.org/2013/03/31/14th-century-the-crash-of-peruzzi-and-the-bardi-fam ily-in-1345/

Financial Innovation Now
https://financialinnovationnow.org/

Financial Markets Toolkit
https://financialmarketstoolkit.cliffordchance.com/en/topic-guides/bank-recovery-and-resolution-directive-brrd.html

Financial Times
"Banks Urge Regulators to Clip Chinese Online Finance Funds." (https://www.ft.com/content/ca8fd57c-9fba-11e3-94f3-00144feab7de)

Equities report. (http://markets.ft.com/data/equities/tearsheet/forecasts?s=BABA:NYQ)
"FT Martin Wolf – Reform of regulation has to start by altering incentives." (https://www.ft.com/content/095722f6-6028-11de-a09b-00144feabdc0)

"In Depth – Big Bang." (https://www.ft.com/content/f3c0d500-8537-11e4-bb63-00144feabdc0)

Financier Worldwide
https://www.financierworldwide.com/the-csmad-significant-imminent-changes-to-eu-market-abuse-and-insider-dealing-rules#.XKika5hKi70

Finovate
https://finovate.com/category/meniga/page/5/

Fintech blog
https://thefintechblog.com/tag/lending-club/
https://thefintechblog.com/tag/prosper/
https://thefintechblog.com/tag/square/

Fintech News
http://fintechnews.sg/26724/philippines/e-wallets-in-the-philippines/

Focus-economics
https://www.focus-economics.com/regions/major-economies

Forbes
"Fintech Innovation Lab in Hong Kong Launches With Eight Firms." (http://www.forbes.com/sites/tomgroenfeldt/2014/09/02/fintech-innovation-lab-in-hong-kong-launches-with-eight-firms/#2b693cdf1ff8)
https://www.forbes.com/companies/robinhood/#4f03b3446076
https://www.forbes.com/sites/julesschroeder/2017/10/31/how-to-tap-into-the-millennial-200-billion-buying-power-with-social-media/#16220e5a1161

Fortune
"How FutureAdvisor plans to shake up wealth management." (http://fortune.com/2014/05/21/how-futureadvisor-plans-to-shake-up-wealth-management)

Fortune, Peter. "Margin Requirements, Margin Loans, and Margin Rates: Practice and Principles – analysis of history of margin credit regulations – Statistical Data Included." *New England Economic Review.*

Fourth Source. "The Digital Strategy Behind the Growth of TransferWise." (http://www.fourthsource.com/general/digital-strategy-behind-growth-transferwise-20447)

Friedman and Schwartz, "Monetary History of the United States." (http://press.princeton.edu/titles/746.html)

Fundera.com
https://www.fundera.com/about

Funding Circle
https://www.fundingcircle.com/

Garanti
https://www.garanti.com.tr/en

Garun, Natt. "Square will launch its Apple Pay-compatible wireless reader this fall." *Next Web.* (http://thenextweb.com/gadgets/2015/06/08/square-will-launch-its-apple-pay-compatible-wireless-reader-this-fall)

Go Compare
https://www.gocompare.com/

Goldthwaite, R. A. "Banks, Places and Entrepreneurs in Renaissance Florence," Aldershot, Hampshire, Great Britain, Variorum.

Google
https://pay.google.com/about/ -

Grabianowski, Ed and Stephanie Crawford. "How PayPal Works." How Stuff Works. (http://money.howstuffworks.com/paypal.htm)

Graven
https://www.graven.co.uk/portfolios/royal-bank-of-scotland-retail-banking-concept/

Guardian
https://www.theguardian.com/world/2018/feb/22/kenya-leads-way-mobile-money-africa-shifts-towards-cash-free-living

Guilford, Gwynn. "China's version of PayPal is mounting one of the biggest challenges to Chinese banks." (http://qz.com/229909/alibaba-now-runs-the-fourth-largest-money-market-fund-in-the-world-and-maybe-the-biggest-challenge-to-chinese-banks)

Hammonds, H. (2006). Banking. North Mankato, MN: Smart Apple Media.

Harvard. "2010 CDO Thesis" (PDF). (http://www.hks.harvard.edu/m-rcbg/students/dunlop/2009-CDOmeltdown.pdf)

The Hill. "Wall Street and the financial crisis: The role of investment banks" (Sen. Carl Levin). (http://thehill.com/blogs/congress-blog/campaign/94549-wall-street-and-the-financial-crisis-the-role-of-investment-banks-sen-carl-levin)

Hoggson, N. F. (1926) "Banking Through the Ages," New York, Dodd, Mead & Company.

Hot Topics. "What is fintech and why does it matter to all entrepreneurs?" (https://www.hottopics.ht/stories/finance/what-is-fintech-and-why-it-matters)

IB Times
https://www.ibtimes.co.uk/bitcoin-now-accepted-by-100000-merchants-worldwide-1486613

Independent
https://www.independent.co.uk/voices/maybe-its-time-for-the-natwest-porcelain-pigs-to-go-to-the-slaughterhouse-a6706497.html

Innovation Enterprise
https://channels.theinnovationenterprise.com/articles/where-are-the-fintech-hubs

Instagram
https://www.instagram.com/lbgtalent/?hl=en

Interaction Awards. "iGaranti – revolutionizing the way we bank." (http://awards.ixda.org/entry/2014/igaranti-revolutionising-the-way-we-bank)

International Fintech
https://internationalfintech.com/Company/money-net/
https://internationalfintech.com/Company/nutmeg/

Int'l. Alipay
https://intl.alipay.com/

Internet World Stats
https://internetworldstats.com/facebook.htm
https://internetworldstats.com/statts.htm

Investopedia
https://www.investopedia.com/terms/p/packaged-retail-investment-and-insurancebased-prod
ucts-priips.asp
https://www.investopedia.com/articles/forex/041515/countries-where-bitcoin-legal-illegal.asp

Irish Times
https://www.irishtimes.com/business/financial-services/contactless-transactions-jump-66-in-
first-half-of-2018-1.3684037

Keaney, M. (2012). Tackling the Financial Crisis. *Political Studies Review*, 10(1), 63–72. (http://dx.
doi.org/10.1111/j.1478-9302.2011.00246.x)

Klebaner, B. J. (1974) "Commercial Banking in the United States: A History," Hinsdale, Illinois,
Dryden Press.

Kindleberger, Charles P. and Robert Aliber (2005). *Manias, Panics, and Crashes: A History of
Financial Crises*, 5th ed. Wiley, ISBN 0-471-46714-6.

KPMG. The Pulse of Fintech, Q1 2016. (https://assets.kpmg.com/content/dam/kpmg/pdf/2016/
05/the-pulse-of-FinTech.pdf)

Laeven, Luc and Fabian Valencia (2008), "Systemic banking crises: a new database." International
Monetary Fund Working Paper 08/224.

Lalwaniildnani, D. Corporate Governance Failure in Financial Services and UK Banking Crisis. SSRN
Electronic Journal. (http://dx.doi.org/10.2139/ssrn.2615619)

LawHKU
https://www.law.hku.hk/faculty/index.php

Legislation.gov
http://www.legislation.gov.uk/ukpga/2009/1/pdfs/ukpga_20090001_en.pdf

Lending Club
https://www.lendingclub.com/

Lendit.com
https://www.lendit.com/usa/2018/sponsors/nomis

Lesonsky, Rieva. "7 Essential Apps for Entrepreneurs." (http://www.readwriteweb.com/start/2012/
07/7-essential-apps-for-entrepreneurs.php)

Let's Talk Payments. "An Average Person used Electronic Payments 260 times per year in this
Country, just as we had Predicted." (https://letstalkpayments.com/average-person-used-elec
tronic-payments-260-times-per-year-country-just-predicted)

Lewis, Lawrence, Jr. (1882). *A History of the Bank of North America, the First Bank Chartered in the
United States*. Philadelphia PA: J. B. Lippincott & Co. pp. 28, 35.

Lewis, Michael (2010). *The Big Short*. W.W. Norton & Company. ISBN 978-0-393-07223-5.

Life Hacker. "Meet Albert, CommBank's New EFTPOS Competitor." (http://www.lifehacker.com.au/2015/03/meet-albert-commbanks-new-eftpos-competitor)

Living History Farm. "Bank Failures." (http://www.livinghistoryfarm.org/farminginthe30s/money_08.html)

Lloyds Bank
https://www.lloydsbankinggroup.com/
https://www.facebook.com/LBGNews/

Luger M. & Evans W. (1988). "Geographic differences in production technology." *Regional Science and Urban Economics*, 18, pp. 339–424.

Macro Trends
https://www.macrotrends.net/stocks/charts/EBAY/ebay/revenue
https://www.macrotrends.net/stocks/charts/PYPL/paypal-holdings/revenue

Market Watch
https://www.marketwatch.com/investing/stock/fb/analystestimates
https://www.marketwatch.com/story/banks-have-been-fined-a-staggering-243-billion-since-the-financial-crisis-2018-02-20

Marous, Jim. "How Will Banks Respond if Apple Becomes Mobile Payments Player," The Financial Brand. (https://thefinancialbrand.com/37233/apple-payments-mobile-wallet-banking-strategy)

McCauley, Daniel. "What is Fintech?" Wharton. (https://medium.com/wharton-fintech/what-is-fintech-77d3d5a3e677#.qx5quer13)

McKinsey. "The rise of the digital bank." (http://www.mckinsey.com/business-functions/digital-mckinsey/our-insights/the-rise-of-the-digital-bank)

McLean, Bethany & Nocera, Joe (2010). *All the Devils Are Here, the Hidden History of the Financial Crisis*, New York: Penguin, p. 120

Medium.com
https://medium.com/@alena.degrik/facebook-pay-is-planning-to-enter-the-eu-market-will-it-launch-in-ukraine-7f9c4c73a27b
https://medium.com/@etiennebr/swish-the-secret-swedish-fintech-payment-company-created-by-nordic-banks-and-used-by-50-of-swedes-cfcf06f59d6f
Meltzer, Allan H. (2003). *A History of the Federal Reserve. Volume 1, 1913–1951*. Chicago: University of Chicago

Meniga
https://www.meniga.com/
https://www.meniga.com/about/
https://blog.meniga.com/measuring-meaningful-engagement-3f8999a98d73

Mfonobong Nsehe. "PayPal Extends Payment Services To Nigeria, 9 Other Countries." *Forbes*. (http://www.forbes.com/sites/mfonobongnsehe/2014/06/17/paypal-extends-payment-services-to-nigeria-9-other-countries/#27129a7c3d0b)

Microbiz. "How Did the Financial Crisis Affect Small Business Lending in the United States." (PDF) (http://www.microbiz.org/wp-content/uploads/2014/04/SBA-SmallBizLending-and-FiscalCrisis.pdf)

Midata
https://www.midata.coop/en/home/
https://midata.io/

Mikesell, Raymond F. The Bretton Woods Debates: A Memoir, Essays in International Finance 192 (Princeton: International Finance Section, Department of Economics, Princeton University)

The Mississippi Bubble
http://www.thebubblebubble.com/mississippi-bubble

M-KESHO
https://ke.equitybankgroup.com/business/products/ways-to-bank/mobile-banking/m-kesho

MobilEarth
https://www.mobilearth.com/mobile-banking-news/digital-transformation-banks-digitization-2018

Mobile Marketer
https://www.mobilemarketer.com/news/facebooks-2018-ad-revenue-surges-38-to-55b-amid-stories-ad-growth/547286/

The Money Cloud Blog. "Meet the $1bn startup changing how we transfer money overseas." (https://www.themoneycloud.com/market-insights/current-events/2015/02/meet-the-$1bn-startup-changing-how-we-transfer-money-oversea)

Money Morning. "Why the Facebook (Nasdaq: FB) Stock Price Will Double by 2018." (http://moneymorning.com/2015/03/05/why-the-facebook-nasdaq-fb-stock-price-will-double-by-2018)

M-PESA
https://mag.n26.com/m-pesa-how-kenya-revolutionized-mobile-payments-56786bc09ef

My Private Banking. "Report: Mobile Apps for Banking 2016." (http://www.myprivatebanking.com/article/report-mobile-apps-for-banking-2016)

NASDAQ
https://www.nasdaq.com/symbol/sq/earnings-growth

Nationwide
https://www.nationwide.com/personal/about-us/newsroom/press-release?title=090214-n-and-eagle

The New York Times
https://www.nytimes.com/2018/11/21/business/sweden-cashless-society.html

Next Web
https://thenextweb.com/facebook/2016/01/27/90-of-facebooks-daily-and-monthly-active-users-access-it-via-mobile/

Norton
https://us.norton.com/internetsecurity-iot-how-facial-recognition-software-works.html

Norton, Rose, Fulbright
https://www.nortonrosefulbright.com/en/knowledge/publications/e78883ef/ten-things-you-need-to-know-about-the-emir-review

OECD
http://www.oecd.org/newsroom/small-business-access-to-alternative-finance-increasing-as-new-bank-lending-declines.htm

Omni Core Agency
https://www.omnicoreagency.com/facebook-statistics/

Orcutt, Mike. "Is Bitcoin Stalling?" *MIT Technology Review*. (https://www.technologyreview.com/s/535221/is-bitcoin-stalling)

Paletta, Damian and Aaron Lucchetti. "Senate Passes Sweeping Finance Overhaul." *Wall Street Journal*. (http://www.wsj.com/articles/SB10001424052748704682604575369030061839958)

Panda Bitcoin. "What is Bitcoin?" (http://www.pandabitcoin.eu)

PayPal. About PayPal.
(https://www.paypal.com/us/webapps/mpp/about)

Paym
https://paym.co.uk/

Payments Journal
https://www.paymentsjournal.com/keeping-an-eye-on-alibaba-ant-financial-and-alipay/

PayPal
(https://www.paypal.com/us/webapps/mpp/about)

Pew Research
https://www.pewresearch.org/fact-tank/2018/04/11/millennials-largest-generation-us-labor-force/

PhilStar. "VMoney redefines the world's payment landscape." philstar.com. (http://www.philstar.com/telecoms/2014/08/16/1357951/vmoney-redefines-worlds-payment-landscape)

Pingit
https://www.pingit.com/

Plaid.com
https://plaid.com/company

Planet Cash
https://en.planetcash.pl/
https://en.planetcash.pl/about-us

Postfunnel
https://postfunnel.com/drives-loyalty-todays-banking-customers/

Price, Rob. "How TransferWise Works." (http://www.businessinsider.com/how-transferwise-works-2015-1)

PSR
https://www.psr.org.uk/

Pymts.com
https://www.pymnts.com/earnings/2018/starbucks-rewards-mobile-app-stocks-loyalty/
https://www.pymnts.com/news/alternative-financial-services/2018/regional-banks-commercial-student-lending-loan-growth-rates/
https://www.pymnts.com/mobile-applications/2018/square-cashed-in-7m-users-for-cash-app/
https://www.pymnts.com/news/payment-methods/2018/square-emv-transactions-chip-cards-mobile-payments/

Quick Pay
https://quickpay.net/payment-methods/vipps

Raab Collection
https://www.raabcollection.com/foreign-figures-autographs/baroncelli-rucellai-renaissance

Rappler. "Empowering the unbanked." (http://www.rappler.com/business/features/71188-executive-edge-vmoney)

Ray, J. Facebook: A Case Study of Strategic Leadership. SSRN Electronic Journal. (http://dx.doi.org/10.2139/ssrn.2103975)

RedHerring. "Fintech Investments Skyrocket in 2016 – Report." (http://www.redherring.com/finance/fintech-investments-skyrocket-2016-report)

Regulation Tomorrow
https://www.regulationtomorrow.com/eu/remuneration-in-crd-iv-firms/

Reuters. "Reuters – info graphics." (http://graphics.thomsonreuters.com/15/bankfines/index.html)
https://www.reuters.com/article/us-bank-branches-idUSKBN17Q28N

Safari
https://www.safaricom.co.ke/

Senate.gov
https://www.hsgac.senate.gov/imo/media/doc/PSI%20REPORT%20-%20Wall%20Street%20&%20the%20Financial%20Crisis-Anatomy%20of%20a%20Financial%20Collapse%20(FINAL%205-10-11).pdf

Shin, Laura. "FinTech 50: The Future of Your Money." Forbes. (http://www.forbes.com/pictures/ghmf45mjkl/the-fintech-50/#6ca767121619)

Simply Pay Group
https://www.simplepaygroup.com/

Singh, Kavaljit. "Fixing Global Finance: A Developing Country Perspective on Global Financial Reforms, Stichting Onderzoek Multinationale Ondernemingen: Centre for Research on Multinational Corporations." (PDF). (http://www.dis.xlibx.info/dd-economy/451662-1-fixing-global-finance-fixi-fixing-global-financ-fixing-loba-fina.php)

SJSU
http://www.sjsu.edu/faculty/watkins/depmon.htm

Skrill
"Proposed Acquisition by Optimal Payments of Skrill to Create Leading Global Player in Online Payment and Digital
"Skrill MasterCard." (http://help.skrill.com/en/Article/business/products-and-services/skrill-card)
"Skrill VIP." (https://www.skrill.com/en/vip-programme

"Skrill MasterCard." (http://help.skrill.com/en/Article/business/products-and-services/skrill-card)

"Skrill VIP." (https://www.skrill.com/en/vip-programme)
https://www.skrill.com/en-us/
https://www.skrill.com/en-us/siteinformation/about-us/

Small Business Administration
https://www.sba.gov/advocacy/small-business-lending-united-states-2016

Smart Asset
https://smartasset.com/checking-account/online-vs-traditional-banks-which-is-better

Sofi.com
https://www.sofi.com/our-story/

Solution Centre
https://www.solutioncentre.ie/

South Sea Company
https://www.amazon.com/s?k=south+sea+company&hvadid=78546414047844&hvbmt=be&hvdev=c&hvqmt=e&tag=mh0b-20&ref=pd_sl_8t6xcew7yc_e

Solutions.refinitiv
http://solutions.refinitiv.com/mifid?utm_content=MiFID%20II-US-AMER-Phrase&utm_medium=cpc&utm_source=bing&utm_campaign=68832_RefinitivBAUPaidSearch&elqCampaignId=5917&utm_term=mifid&msclkid=4eab1b8288d5164fd357472a2d884e00

Sparkes, Matthew. "The coming digital anarchy." *The Telegraph*. http://www.telegraph.co.uk/technology/news/10881213/The-coming-digital-anarchy.html)

Springer
https://link.springer.com/article/10.1007/BF01581896

SRB Europa
https://srb.europa.eu/en/content/single-resolution-mechanism-srm

SSRN
https://papers.ssrn.com/sol3/papers.cfm?abstract_id=2676553

Statista
https://www.statista.com/statistics/412056/global-investment-in-fintech-companies/
https://www.statista.com/statistics/558221/number-of-facebook-users-in-china/
https://www.statista.com/statistics/298844/net-income-alibaba/
https://www.statista.com/statistics/663622/credit-card-usage-in-sweden/

The Star
https://www.the-star.co.ke/news/2018-11-06-safaricom-western-union-launch-m-pesa-global-in-over-200-countries/

Stockholm School of Economics. "Stockholm FinTech: An overview of the FinTech sector in the greater Stockholm Region." (PDF). – https://www.hhs.se/contentassets/b5823453b8fe4290828fcc81189b6561/stockholm-fintech—june-2015.pdf

The Street. "Square Surges as Analysts Point to Brighter Growth Prospects." (https://www.thestreet.com/story/13683138/2/square-surges-as-analysts-point-to-brighter-growth-prospects.html)

Square
"Free Credit Card Reader." (https://squareup.com/reader)

"Square's Fees."
https://squareup.com/help/us/en/article/5068-square-s-payment-processing-fees-and-pricing

Stanford. "Financial Crisis Inquiry Commission – story of a security." (http://fcic.law.stanford.edu/resource/staff-data-projects/story-of-a-security)

Stripe.com
https://stripe.com/about

SWIFT. "SWIFT History." (https://www.swift.com/about-us/discover-swift)

Tata
https://www.tcs.com/

Tech Target
https://whatis.techtarget.com/definition/center-of-excellence-CoE

TFL.gov
https://tfl.gov.uk/info-for/media/press-releases/2017/july/one-billion-journeys-made-by-contactless-payment-on-london-s-transport-network

This American Life. NPR. "The Giant Pool of Money" (Radio). (http://www.thisamericanlife.org/radio-archives/episode/355/the-giant-pool-of-money)

This Is Money
https://www.thisismoney.co.uk/money/saving/article-4946222/Don-t-details-new-money-apps-says-NatWest.html

Transact. "The Rise of Digital Banking." (http://www.transact.org.uk/news.aspx?itemid=2425&itemTitle=The±Rise±of±Digital±Banking&sitesectionid=29&sitesectiontitle=News)

TransferWise.
"The Future of Finance." (https://transferwise.com/gb/blog/how-technology-is-democratising-the-financial-services-sector)

"The impact on the financial sector." (https://transferwise.com/gb/blog/the-impact-on-the-financial-sector-the-democratisation-of-finance)

"The Unbundling of The Banks." (https://transferwise.com/gb/blog/the-unbundling-of-banks-2)
https://transferwise.com/us
https://transferwise.com/us/about/our-story
https://transferwise.com/us

Treasury Department
https://occ.treas.gov/topics/compliance-bsa/bsa/index-bsa.html

USAA
https://mobile.usaa.com/inet/wc/usaa_mobile_main?akredirect=true

Venture Beat. "Amazon Web Services is now a $5B business." (http://venturebeat.com/2015/04/23/amazon-web-services-is-now-a-5b-business)

Wall Street Journal
"Alibaba Expects 48% Revenue Growth in First Forecast." (http://www.wsj.com/articles/alibaba-says-closely-watched-sales-metric-may-not-remain-the-standard-1465877128)
https://www.wsj.com/articles/regional-banks-brush-off-yield-curve-worries-11547683841

Wallet Services
(https://content.skrill.com/en-us/about-us/press/details/proposed-acquisition-by-optimal-payments-of-skrill-to-create-leading-global-player-in-online-payment)

Wealthfront.com
https://www.wealthfront.com/

Welab
https://www.welab.co/en

Westlaw Journal Computer and Internet. "Criminalizing Free Enterprise: The Bank Secrecy Act and the Cryptocurrency Revolution."

Westpac
https://www.westpac.com.au/

Wharton Fintech
https://www.whartonfintech.org/

The White House. "Obama-Regulatory Reform Speech June 17, 2009." (https://www.whitehouse.gov/the-press-office/remarks-president-regulatory-reform)

Wikipedia
https://en.wikipedia.org/wiki/List_of_largest_financial_services_companies_by_revenue

Williams, Carol J. "Euro crisis imperils recovering global economy, OECD warns." *Los Angeles Times*. (http://latimesblogs.latimes.com/world_now/2012/05/eurozone-crisis-global-economy.html)

Wolf, Martin (June 23, 2009). "Reform of regulation has to start by altering incentives." FT.com

Working Media Group
https://www.workingmediagroup.com/why-millennials-are-leaving-your-bank-and-how-to-stop-them/

World Bank
https://www.imf.org/en/About/Factsheets/Sheets/2016/07/27/15/31/IMF-World-Bank
"The bursting of the U.S." http://blogs.worldbank.org/allaboutfinance/comment/reply/880/1246
https://www.worldbank.org/en/news/feature/2018/10/03/what-kenya-s-mobile-money-success-could-mean-for-the-arab-world
https://data.worldbank.org/indicator/FB.ATM.TOTL.P5

WorldPay "Global Online Shopper Report," (http://www.worldpay.com/global/insight/articles/2014-12/global-online-shopper)

YCharts
https://ycharts.com/companies/FB/market_cap

Thank you

Thank you so much for reading this book. We hope that you have found it both enjoyable to read as well as useful! We are currently living through a fascinating period for the banking industry, where for the first time the financial customer is being put first with innovations being developed around what consumers have long expected of their financial service provider. This current digital era has not only empowered today's customers to be more in control of their finances, but it has also dramatically increased the number of ways in which financial institutions can now interact with their clients.

With big data analytics, retail banks can know more about their customers, as well as potential clients than at any other time in banking history. The application of these analytics to distill raw data into meaningful insight is now prevalent among all large financial institutions. With all of them regularly acting on insights gleaned from transactional and interactional behavior of their customers, thus enabling curated products and specific services to be offered digitally and instantly.

We believe that the future holds many more exciting financial innovations, especially due to the battle lines having already been drawn for what will be an enthralling showdown between retail banks and fintech companies, with each trying to outdo the other.

Please feel free to contact us via email:

info@digitalbankingrevolution.com or alternatively follow me
on Twitter: @luigiwewege

Thomsett1948@yahoo.com
or on Twitter: @ThomsettPublish

https://doi.org/10.1515/9781547401598-013

Index

https://doi.org/10.1515/9781547401598-014

CPSIA information can be obtained
at www.ICGtesting.com
Printed in the USA
JSHW040749081220
10043JS00006B/78

9 781547 418336